UTOPALIS

KAYAN

UTOPALIS

Kayan
UTOPALIS

Published by Spines
ISBN: 979-8-89691-098-5

CONTENTS

INTRODUCTION

In the 21st century, the world is grappling with an array of challenges that test the resilience of both individuals and societies. Climate change, once a distant concern, now directly impacts ecosystems, economies, and the well-being of populations across the globe. Rising temperatures, natural disasters, and resource depletion force us to confront the fragile relationship between humanity and the planet. Social instability has become a hallmark of our times, as political polarization, cultural fragmentation, and widespread disillusionment create divides that undermine our collective ability to address pressing global issues. Economic disparity continues to grow, as the gap between the wealthy and the rest widens, eroding the foundations of opportunity and fairness that once promised upward mobility for all.

In addition to these external challenges, our inner worlds are also in turmoil. Decreased birth rates in many parts of the world reflect shifting priorities, economic pressures, and uncertainties about the future. Simultaneously, high levels of depression and anxiety reveal a deep sense of dissatisfaction and disconnection within modern life. Despite unprecedented technological advances and access to information, many find themselves unfulfilled, questioning the purpose and meaning of their existence. Life satisfaction, once a core pursuit of human beings, seems elusive in a world overwhelmed by materialism, competition, and the erosion of communal bonds.

These intersecting crises raise a fundamental question: How did we arrive at this point? To understand the roots of these issues, we must look back at the development of the societal structures that have shaped human civilization. Over millennia, humans have built systems of governance, economics, family, and culture, all intended to create stability, order, and opportunity. These structures, while evolving to meet the needs of their times, have also been shaped by historical circumstances, ideologies, and power dynamics that often overlooked the individual's pursuit of meaning and fulfillment. While we benefit from many aspects of these systems today, it is clear that they are no longer sufficient to address the profound shifts in human consciousness, technological advancement, and global interconnectedness that define our current era.

The time has come to critically examine these structures—not only to understand their evolution but also to learn from their successes and failures. By reflecting on the development of societal institutions, such as the family, economy, education, and governance, we can identify the lessons that have been gathered over time. These lessons offer valuable insights into how we can build a more adaptive, inclusive, and humane society moving forward. A society that respects the dignity and autonomy of every individual, while also fostering a sense of communal responsibility and collective well-being.

Central to this exploration is the recognition that the systems and institutions of today must be reimagined for the future. The old ways of organizing society, rooted in hierarchical structures, rigid economic models, and exclusionary practices, have outlived their usefulness. We are entering an era where flexibility, inclusivity, and holistic well-being must take precedence. This requires not only a shift in how we design societal frameworks but also a transformation in how we understand the role of individuals within those frameworks. The individual, long viewed as a cog in the machine of larger social structures, must now be placed at the center of our considerations. A system that genuinely serves humanity must recognize and support the intrinsic value of each person, ensuring that they have the opportunity to live a life of purpose, connection, and fulfillment.

The journey to a more equitable and fulfilling society will not be easy. It will require a rethinking of deeply ingrained assumptions about the nature of human existence, progress, and success. It will challenge us to confront uncomfortable truths about how we have historically marginalized certain groups, prioritized short-term gains over long-term sustainability, and allowed systems of power to perpetuate inequality. But it is a journey worth embarking on, for the stakes could not be higher. The future of humanity depends on our ability to build structures that are not only efficient and productive but also compassionate, just, and capable of nurturing the full potential of each individual.

This book is a reflection on that journey. It will explore the historical evolution of the institutions we rely on today, from the family unit to economic and political systems. It will examine the ways in which these structures have shaped, and at times constrained, human flourishing. And it will propose new ways of thinking about organization, community, and identity that are more attuned to the needs of modern life. By synthesizing lessons from the past with the realities of the present, this book aims to offer a blueprint for a future society that can meet the challenges of our time while fostering a sense of prosperity and fulfillment for all.

Ultimately, this is a call to action. It is time to take the accumulated wisdom of history and use it to forge a new path forward—a path that honors the dignity of every individual, promotes the common good, and ensures that the systems we create serve humanity, rather than the other way around. By reimagining the structures of society, we can build a world where prosperity and fulfillment are not just aspirations but realities for everyone.

DEVELOPMENT OF HUMANISTIC SYSTEMS: A HISTORICAL OVERVIEW

Throughout history, human societies have evolved by developing systems that respond to the needs of survival, organization, and mutual benefit. These humanistic systems— shaped by socio-political, socio-economic, and organizational imperatives—form the foundation of civilization as we know it today. The evolution of these systems reveals the complexity of human relationships, the drive for cooperation, and the constant tension between individual desires and collective needs.

Socio-Political Development

The earliest forms of socio-political organization were tribal and kin-based, where leadership was often determined by strength, wisdom, or spiritual authority. These small groups relied on cooperation for survival, and decisions were often made communally or through tribal leaders. As societies grew larger and more complex, so too did the need for more structured forms of governance. Early civilizations such as Mesopotamia, Ancient Egypt, and the Indus Valley developed centralized forms of governance, often led by monarchs, who were seen as divinely sanctioned rulers with absolute authority.

The Greeks, however, introduced the concept of democracy, particularly in Athens, where citizens could directly participate in decision-making. This marked a significant shift toward the idea that individuals could influence their governance. Similarly, the Roman Republic provided a model for representative governance, a structure that would inspire future political systems.

Over centuries, monarchies, empires, and later, nation-states emerged, often using a combination of centralized power and advisory councils or parliaments. The Enlightenment of the 17th and 18th centuries sparked a more radical shift in socio-political thought, leading to the rise of constitutional democracy, the separation of powers, and the concept of human rights. These developments laid the groundwork for modern governance, as societies sought to balance authority with individual freedoms.

Socio-Economic Development

Early economies were simple, based on bartering and trading goods within small communities. People exchanged resources such as food, tools, and services, with value determined largely by immediate need and availability. However, as societies became more complex and populations expanded, the limitations of barter systems became apparent. This led to the development of early forms of currency, such as grain, livestock, and eventually precious metals like gold and silver, which became standardized mediums of exchange.

The rise of agriculture significantly transformed economic systems. As humans settled into farming communities, surplus production became possible, leading to the creation of more stratified economies. Societies began to accumulate wealth, and systems of trade expanded beyond local communities to include far-reaching trade networks. The Silk Road, for example, connected the economies of Europe, the Middle East, and Asia, facilitating the exchange of goods, cultures, and ideas.

The Industrial Revolution in the 18th and 19th centuries marked a pivotal moment in socio-economic development. Mechanization revolutionized production, leading to the rise of capitalist economies where private ownership, competition, and profit motive dominated. This shift brought unprecedented economic growth, but also significant inequality and exploitation, as seen in the harsh conditions faced by many laborers in industrial factories. The development of socialist and communist ideologies arose in response, advocating for the redistribution of wealth and collective ownership of resources.

Today's global economy, driven by advanced technology and multinational corporations, continues to evolve rapidly. The rise of digital currencies, automation, and artificial intelligence are transforming how people work, trade, and engage in economic activity, challenging existing systems and sparking debates about the future of work and wealth distribution.

Organizational Development

Human organization has progressed from loose, tribal associations to more complex forms of collective endeavor. In the earliest societies, social organization was relatively simple, based on familial and tribal bonds. As groups grew larger, more structured forms of organization emerged to manage agriculture, resource distribution, and defense. These early organizational structures laid the foundation for modern systems of governance and economics.

In ancient civilizations, centralized bureaucracies and hierarchies helped rulers maintain control over large territories and populations. Religious institutions often played a key role in organizational development, as priestly classes provided both spiritual leadership and administrative functions. Feudalism in the Middle Ages represented another form of socio-political organization, where land ownership and military service were the basis for societal structure.

The Renaissance and the Enlightenment brought a wave of intellectual and organizational transformations. The scientific method introduced new ways of organizing knowledge, while early capitalist enterprises, such as joint-stock companies, represented a new way to organize economic production and risk. This period also saw the birth of formal education systems and legal frameworks designed to regulate society.

In the modern era, organizations have become more specialized and diverse. From corporations and non-profit organizations to international institutions such as the United Nations, the organizational landscape reflects a broad array of human needs and goals. Technological advancement has further enabled the growth of decentralized, flexible organizations that operate across borders, driving new forms of economic and social cooperation.

Development of Mediums of Exchange

As societies grew in complexity, so did their methods of exchanging goods and services. Early humans bartered goods directly, but as communities grew, this system became inefficient. Early forms of currency emerged as societies sought more standardized methods of trade.

Initially, items such as livestock, grains, or other goods of intrinsic value were used as currency. Over time, metal objects —particularly precious metals like gold and silver—became preferred due to their durability, divisibility, and portability. Ancient civilizations, including the Greeks and Romans, minted coins as a more formalized medium of exchange, assigning specific value to standardized pieces of metal.

The introduction of paper money in China during the Tang and Song dynasties revolutionized trade. Paper was easier to transport than metal, and the concept of promissory notes laid the foundation for modern banking. By the 17th century, European economies began issuing their own forms of paper money, which eventually became the dominant medium of exchange globally.

In the 20th century, the gold standard—which tied currency value directly to gold—was largely abandoned, replaced by fiat currency, money that has no intrinsic value but is backed by government regulation. Today's financial systems, including the rise of digital currencies and decentralized blockchain technology, continue to push the boundaries of how we conceptualize and use mediums of exchange.

WHAT IS JUSTICE?

Introduction

Justice is a fundamental concept that underpins societal values, legal systems, and ethical frameworks. It embodies the principles of fairness, equality, and moral righteousness, guiding how individuals and institutions interact and make decisions. This chapter explores the concept of justice, examining its philosophical foundations, various interpretations, and its application in different contexts.

Philosophical Foundations of Justice

Ancient Philosophies

Justice has been a central theme in philosophical discourse since ancient times. Greek philosophers such as Plato and Aristotle laid the groundwork for Western understandings of justice.

- **Plato:** In "The Republic," Plato describes justice as a harmonious structure where each part of society performs its appropriate role. He emphasizes the importance of a just society where individuals act according to their abilities and societal needs.
- **Aristotle:** Aristotle, in "Nicomachean Ethics," defines justice as giving each person their due. He distinguishes between distributive justice (fair allocation of resources) and corrective justice (rectification of wrongs).

Enlightenment Thinkers

During the Enlightenment, philosophers like John Locke, Jean-Jacques Rousseau, and Immanuel Kant further developed the concept of justice.

- **John Locke:** Locke's theories of natural rights and social contract emphasize individual rights and the protection of property as central to justice.
- **Jean-Jacques Rousseau:** Rousseau's "The Social Contract" posits that justice arises from the collective will of the people, aiming for the common good.
- **Immanuel Kant:** Kant's deontological ethics highlight the role of moral duties and the inherent dignity of individuals, framing justice as respecting and upholding the rights of all.

Interpretations of Justice

Distributive Justice

Distributive justice concerns the fair allocation of resources and opportunities within society. It addresses questions of who should get what and why.

- **Egalitarianism:** Egalitarians advocate for equal distribution of resources and opportunities, emphasizing that everyone should have the same starting point.
- **Utilitarianism:** Utilitarians focus on maximizing overall happiness and welfare, advocating for resource distribution that benefits the greatest number of people.
- **Libertarianism:** Libertarians prioritize individual freedom and property rights, arguing that justice is achieved when individuals are free to acquire and use resources without coercive interference.

Procedural Justice

Procedural justice emphasizes fairness in the processes and methods used to make decisions and resolve disputes. Key principles include:

- **Transparency:** Decision-making processes should be open and transparent, allowing all parties to understand how decisions are made.
- **Impartiality:** Decisions should be made impartially, without bias or favoritism.

- **Participation:** Individuals affected by decisions should have the opportunity to participate in the process and voice their concerns.

Retributive Justice

Retributive justice focuses on the fair punishment of wrongdoers. It is based on the principle that those who commit injustices deserve to be punished proportionally to their offenses.

- **Proportionality:** Punishments should be proportional to the severity of the wrongdoing.
- **Deterrence:** Punishments should deter future wrongdoing by discouraging individuals from committing offenses.
- **Restitution:** Offenders should make amends to their victims, restoring what was lost or damaged.

Restorative Justice

Restorative justice emphasizes repairing harm caused by wrongdoing through reconciliation and rehabilitation rather than punishment.

- **Victim-Centered:** Focuses on addressing the needs and rights of victims, providing them with a voice in the justice process.
- **Rehabilitation:** Aims to rehabilitate offenders and reintegrate them into society.
- **Community Involvement:** Involves the community in

the justice process, fostering a sense of collective responsibility and healing.

Applications of Justice

Legal Systems

Justice is a cornerstone of legal systems, guiding the creation, interpretation, and enforcement of laws.

- **Rule of Law:** The principle that all individuals and institutions are subject to the law, ensuring fairness and accountability.
- **Judicial Independence:** Courts must be independent and impartial, making decisions based on the law and evidence without external influence.

Social Justice

Social justice addresses systemic inequalities and aims to create a fair and equitable society.

- **Economic Justice:** Focuses on reducing economic disparities and ensuring fair access to resources and opportunities.
- **Racial and Gender Justice:** Seeks to eliminate discrimination and promote equality for marginalized groups based on race, gender, and other identities.
- **Environmental Justice:** Advocates for the fair distribution of environmental benefits and burdens, ensuring that all communities have access to a healthy environment.

Global Justice

Global justice extends the principles of fairness and equality to the international arena, addressing issues such as:

- **Human Rights:** Protecting and promoting fundamental human rights for all individuals, regardless of nationality.
- **International Trade:** Ensuring fair and equitable trade practices that do not exploit developing countries.
- **Global Inequality:** Addressing disparities between nations in terms of wealth, health, and access to resources.

THE CHALLENGE OF CREATING A JUST SOCIETY

Creating a just society, where fairness, equality, and human rights are upheld for all, is a fundamental aspiration of modern governance and social development. However, achieving this ideal presents numerous challenges. This chapter explores the multifaceted obstacles to establishing a just society, examining issues related to economic inequality, social justice, political governance, cultural diversity, and global interdependence.

Economic Inequality

Wealth Disparities

One of the primary challenges in creating a just society is addressing economic inequality. Wealth disparities result in unequal access to resources, opportunities, and services. These disparities can perpetuate cycles of poverty and limit social mobility, making it difficult for individuals from disadvantaged backgrounds to improve their economic status.

Access to Education and Employment

Education and employment opportunities are critical for reducing economic inequality. However, systemic barriers often prevent equal access to quality education and job opportunities. Addressing these barriers requires comprehensive policies that promote inclusive education, skill development, and equitable labor markets.

Social Justice

Discrimination and Prejudice

Discrimination and prejudice based on race, gender, ethnicity, religion, and other social identities are significant obstacles to social justice. These biases can manifest in various forms, including institutional discrimination, social exclusion, and unequal treatment under the law. Combatting discrimination requires robust anti-discrimination laws, education, and cultural change.

Legal and Institutional Frameworks

Creating a just society necessitates strong legal and institutional frameworks that uphold human rights and ensure equal protection under the law. However, existing legal systems may be biased or ineffective in addressing the needs of marginalized communities. Reforms are needed to ensure that legal institutions are fair, transparent, and accountable.

Political Governance

Corruption and Accountability

Corruption undermines the principles of justice and fairness by enabling the misuse of power for personal gain. It erodes public trust in institutions and disproportionately affects the most vulnerable. Ensuring accountability through transparent governance, strong anti-corruption measures, and active civil society participation is essential for building a just society.

Representation and Participation

Inclusive political participation is crucial for a just society. However, marginalized groups often face barriers to political representation and participation. Ensuring that all voices are heard requires electoral reforms, inclusive political practices, and the empowerment of underrepresented communities.

Cultural Diversity

Social Cohesion and Integration

Cultural diversity enriches societies but can also pose challenges for social cohesion and integration. Balancing respect for cultural differences with the promotion of shared values is essential for maintaining harmony in diverse societies. Policies that promote intercultural dialogue, social inclusion, and mutual respect are vital.

Identity and Belonging

A just society must ensure that all individuals feel a sense of identity and belonging. This involves recognizing and valuing diverse cultural identities while fostering a shared national identity. Addressing issues of identity and belonging requires inclusive policies and practices that celebrate diversity and promote social unity.

Global Interdependence

International Inequality

Global inequality poses a significant challenge to justice at both national and international levels. Disparities in wealth, resources, and opportunities between countries can perpetuate global poverty and hinder development. Addressing international inequality requires collaborative efforts, fair trade practices, and support for sustainable development initiatives.

Human Rights and Global Governance

Protecting human rights in a globally interconnected world requires effective global governance. However, international institutions often face challenges in enforcing human rights standards and addressing transnational issues. Strengthening global governance frameworks and ensuring international cooperation are critical for promoting justice worldwide.

Environmental Justice

Climate Change and Resource Management

Environmental justice is an integral aspect of a just society. Climate change and resource mismanagement disproportionately affect vulnerable populations, exacerbating inequality and injustice. Policies that promote sustainable development, equitable resource distribution, and climate resilience are essential for environmental justice.

Access to Clean Air, Water, and Land

Ensuring access to clean air, water, and land is fundamental for a just society. Environmental degradation and pollution often impact marginalized communities the most. Addressing these issues requires stringent environmental regulations, community engagement, and equitable resource management practices.

Social Policy and Welfare

Social Safety Nets

Robust social safety nets are crucial for supporting vulnerable populations and promoting social justice. However, designing and implementing effective welfare programs can be challenging. Ensuring that social safety nets are inclusive, sustainable, and responsive to changing needs is essential for a just society.

Healthcare Access

Universal access to quality healthcare is a cornerstone of social justice. Health disparities and unequal access to medical services can perpetuate inequality and hinder social progress. Policies that promote universal healthcare coverage, address health disparities, and ensure affordable access to medical services are vital.

Education and Empowerment

Equitable Education Systems

Education is a powerful tool for achieving social justice. Equitable education systems that provide quality learning opportunities for all, regardless of socioeconomic background, are essential. This requires addressing disparities in educational resources, facilities, and opportunities.

Empowerment and Agency

Empowering individuals to take control of their lives and make informed decisions is fundamental for a just society. This involves promoting education, awareness, and capacity-building initiatives that enable people to advocate for their rights and participate fully in societal development.

Conclusion

Creating a just society is a complex and multifaceted challenge that requires addressing economic inequality, promoting social justice, ensuring inclusive governance, respecting cultural diversity, and fostering global cooperation. It involves tackling systemic issues and implementing comprehensive policies that promote fairness, equity, and human rights. While the path to a just society is fraught with challenges, understanding these obstacles is the first step toward overcoming them. By embracing inclusive and equitable practices, fostering collaboration, and upholding the principles of justice, societies can move closer to achieving this fundamental aspiration.

SOCIO-ECONOMIC SYSTEMS

HISTORY OF COMMUNISM AND SOCIALISM

Socialism and communism share roots in the 19th-century critique of industrial capitalism, both advocating for the collective ownership of resources and the means of production. However, while socialism encompasses a broad range of political and economic ideologies aiming to reduce inequality, communism, as defined by Karl Marx and Friedrich Engels, is a more radical form, envisioning a classless, stateless society.

Early Socialism

The intellectual foundations of socialism can be traced to thinkers like Henri de Saint-Simon, Charles Fourier, and Robert Owen, often referred to as utopian socialists. They critiqued the social and economic inequalities caused by industrial capitalism and proposed cooperative communities where wealth was distributed more evenly. These early socialist movements focused on reform and voluntary cooperation rather than revolution.

It was Karl Marx and Friedrich Engels, however, who gave socialism its more revolutionary character. In their seminal work, *The Communist Manifesto* (1848), they laid the groundwork for what would later become communism. Marx's theory of historical materialism argued that all of history was a struggle between classes, with capitalism merely a stage in this progression. He predicted that the working class (proletariat) would eventually overthrow the capitalist class (bourgeoisie) and create a society based on communal ownership, thus eliminating class divisions.

Rise of Communism

While socialism began as a reformist movement in Western Europe, communism took a different trajectory. Following the 1917 Russian Revolution, the Bolsheviks, led by Vladimir Lenin, established the first communist state. Marx's vision of a global revolution began to take shape, and Lenin adapted Marxist theory to suit Russian conditions, arguing for a "vanguard party" to lead the working class to power. After Lenin's death, Joseph Stalin's authoritarian rule marked a shift towards totalitarianism. His policies of rapid industrialization and collectivization had both disastrous and transformative effects, including massive famines but also the transformation of the Soviet Union into a superpower.

The Soviet model of communism spread to Eastern Europe after World War II and influenced revolutions in Asia, Latin America, and Africa. The Chinese Communist Revolution, led by Mao Zedong in 1949, resulted in the People's Republic of

China, which implemented its own form of Marxist-Leninist policies. Mao's radical policies, such as the Great Leap Forward and the Cultural Revolution, would later contribute to significant social and economic upheaval.

Meanwhile, socialism in Western Europe and other regions took on a more moderate form. After World War II, many European countries adopted socialist-inspired policies, including welfare states, labor protections, and nationalized industries. These policies, known as social democracy, sought to balance capitalism with social safety nets.

Successes of Communism and Socialism

1. Reduction of Inequality

One of the primary achievements of socialist and communist states was the reduction of income inequality. Through state ownership of industries and redistribution of wealth, these systems aimed to ensure that basic needs such as housing, healthcare, and education were available to all. For example, during the Soviet era, education and healthcare were free and widely accessible, providing upward mobility for many.

2. Rapid Industrialization

The Soviet Union, under Stalin, experienced rapid industrial growth, transforming from a largely agrarian society into a global superpower within a few decades. This industrial growth, often driven by centralized planning and large-scale state-led projects, played a significant role in the Soviet Union's ability to compete on the global stage, particularly during the Cold War.

3. Improvements in Literacy and Public Health

Communist and socialist regimes often prioritized education and public health. Cuba, under Fidel Castro's communist government, has achieved one of the highest literacy rates and some of the best healthcare outcomes in the developing world, despite economic sanctions and resource limitations. Similar progress was seen in Eastern European countries and parts of Asia.

4. Mobilization of Resources

Centralized planning allowed communist states to mobilize resources on a large scale for specific projects, whether for industrial development or military buildup. This capacity enabled the Soviet Union, China, and other countries to quickly rebuild after wars or other disasters, though often at a high human cost.

5. Women's Rights and Gender Equality

Many communist and socialist states made significant strides in promoting gender equality. In the Soviet Union and China, women were encouraged to participate in the workforce, and gender discrimination was legally prohibited. State-run childcare, maternity leave, and equal pay policies were implemented to support working women.

Failures of Communism and Socialism

1. Authoritarianism and Lack of Political Freedom

One of the most notable failures of communist regimes was their tendency toward authoritarianism. The Soviet Union, under Stalin, experienced purges, forced labor camps, and widespread surveillance. Similar patterns emerged in Maoist China, North Korea, and Eastern Bloc countries. In many cases, dissent was crushed, and citizens had little to no political freedom. The promise of a "classless society" often led to the rise of new elite classes, entrenched in political power.

2. Economic Inefficiency

Centralized planning often resulted in economic inefficiencies. Without the market signals of supply and demand, socialist economies struggled to allocate resources efficiently. For instance, the Soviet Union's planned economy resulted in chronic shortages of consumer goods and low-quality products. The absence of competition and incentives for innovation stifled economic growth in many communist states.

3. Human Rights Abuses

Many communist regimes were responsible for widespread human rights abuses. Stalin's purges, Mao's Great Leap Forward and Cultural Revolution, and the Khmer Rouge in Cambodia led to the deaths of millions through executions, forced labor, and starvation. These human rights abuses were often justified in the name of creating an egalitarian society but resulted in immense suffering and loss of life.

4. Collapse of the Soviet Union and Economic Failure

The Soviet Union's collapse in 1991 marked the failure of the most prominent communist state. Economic stagnation, the inefficiencies of central planning, and an unsustainable arms race with the United States contributed to the Soviet Union's downfall. This collapse highlighted the difficulties of maintaining a communist state over the long term, particularly in the face of growing global capitalism.

5. Lack of Innovation and Entrepreneurship

Socialist and communist systems, by their nature, discouraged private ownership and entrepreneurship, which are often engines of innovation. Without competitive pressures and incentives to innovate, many communist economies lagged behind capitalist ones in technological and industrial development. This stifling of individual initiative led to economic stagnation in countries like the Soviet Union and North Korea.

6. Failed Agricultural Policies

Collectivization of agriculture, as seen in the Soviet Union under Stalin and in China under Mao, resulted in disastrous famines. In both countries, millions died as a result of poor planning, forced collectivization, and mismanagement of agricultural resources. The lack of private incentives to increase productivity also meant that many socialist economies were unable to feed their populations adequately.

Conclusion

While socialism and communism were born from noble ideals of equality, fairness, and collective well-being, their implementation in practice often revealed significant flaws. In the communist states, the concentration of political power in the hands of the few often led to authoritarian regimes and human rights abuses, while economic inefficiency plagued centralized systems. However, successes in education, healthcare, and the reduction of inequality, particularly in some socialist systems, demonstrate that aspects of these ideologies have lasting value.

HISTORY OF CAPITALISM

Capitalism, the economic system where private individuals or businesses own capital goods, has developed over centuries and now dominates much of the global economy. The core principles of capitalism include private property, capital accumulation, wage labor, voluntary exchange, and competitive markets. Unlike socialism or communism, capitalism emphasizes the role of the individual in pursuing wealth and economic gain, often with minimal state intervention.

Early Capitalism

The roots of capitalism can be traced back to the late Middle Ages in Europe, particularly in Italy, where cities like Venice and Florence became centers of trade and finance. During this time, merchants and traders accumulated wealth through commercial ventures, often backed by early forms of banking and financial services. As European nations expanded globally through colonialism in the 15th and 16th centuries, capitalism began to take on a more international scope. The development of trade routes and mercantilism (a form of economic nationalism) helped European powers build vast empires and wealth by exploiting foreign markets and resources.

The Industrial Revolution in the 18th and 19th centuries was a turning point for capitalism. Mechanized production, driven by technological innovation, led to unprecedented economic growth. Britain became the birthplace of modern capitalism, where entrepreneurs like James Watt and industrialists like Andrew Carnegie helped shape the new industrial economy. Factories, urbanization, and mass production were central to this transformation, and capitalists (owners of the means of production) benefited from the profits generated by laborers, who often worked under harsh conditions for low wages.

The Rise of Free Market Capitalism

The rise of free market economics in the 18th century, notably through the work of Adam Smith and his book *The Wealth of Nations* (1776), provided the theoretical foundation for capitalism. Smith argued that individuals, by pursuing their self-interest, inadvertently benefit society as a whole. He introduced the concept of the "invisible hand," suggesting that free markets regulate themselves through competition, supply and demand, and the pursuit of profit. Smith's ideas would influence economic policies throughout the 19th and 20th centuries, particularly the promotion of laissez-faire (minimal government intervention) capitalism.

Capitalism continued to evolve in the 19th and early 20th centuries with the expansion of industrial economies, the rise of multinational corporations, and the financialization of markets. While some capitalist countries embraced free-market policies, others experimented with more interventionist approaches, particularly in the aftermath of economic crises.

Successes of Capitalism

1. Economic Growth and Innovation

One of the greatest successes of capitalism has been its ability to drive innovation and economic growth. The competitive nature of capitalist economies incentivizes individuals and businesses to find more efficient ways to produce goods and services. This drive for innovation has led to technological advancements that have transformed industries and improved the quality of life for millions. The Industrial Revolution, for example, radically changed production methods and allowed economies to grow rapidly.

2. Rising Standards of Living

Capitalism has contributed to significant improvements in standards of living across the world. As economies grow, wealth is created, and people have access to better goods and services, healthcare, education, and infrastructure. Over time, capitalist economies have reduced extreme poverty, expanded access to education, and improved life expectancy. Many of the world's wealthiest countries, such as the United States and members of the European Union, owe their prosperity to capitalist principles.

3. Global Trade and Economic Integration

Capitalism has played a crucial role in the development of global trade and economic integration. By opening markets and reducing trade barriers, capitalism has created a global economy where goods, services, and capital can flow more freely across borders. Globalization has been driven by capitalist economies, facilitating access to foreign markets and fostering economic growth in developing countries. Free trade has allowed countries to specialize in producing goods where they have a competitive advantage, increasing global efficiency and productivity.

4. Consumer Choice

Capitalism fosters consumer choice by creating a diverse marketplace with a wide range of products and services. In competitive markets, businesses must innovate and improve to attract consumers, leading to more options and better quality goods. This competition benefits consumers by lowering prices and increasing the availability of products that suit different tastes and needs. The tech industry, with its constant cycle of innovation and product development, is a prime example of this dynamic.

5. Wealth Creation

Capitalism has been extraordinarily successful in creating wealth. The accumulation of capital, investment in businesses, and stock markets have enabled individuals to amass significant fortunes. Entrepreneurs, through risk-taking and innovation, can build large enterprises that generate wealth not only for themselves but for shareholders, employees, and the broader economy. The U.S. and many Western economies have experienced sustained wealth generation due to capitalist systems.

Failures of Capitalism

1. Income Inequality

One of the most significant criticisms of capitalism is its tendency to generate large disparities in wealth and income. While capitalism has created immense wealth, it has also concentrated that wealth in the hands of a small minority, often leading to extreme income inequality. The "1%" versus "99%" debate highlights how the wealthiest individuals and corporations can accumulate vast resources while large sections of the population struggle to meet basic needs. In many capitalist economies, income inequality has worsened, especially in the late 20th and early 21st centuries, contributing to social unrest.

2. Economic Crises

Capitalist economies are prone to cycles of boom and bust, leading to periodic economic crises that can have devastating effects on society. The Great Depression of the 1930s and the 2008 global financial crisis are two prominent examples of how speculative bubbles and deregulation in capitalist economies can lead to widespread economic hardship. In both cases, millions of people lost their jobs, homes, and savings due to systemic failures in capitalist financial systems. These crises also revealed the inherent instability of unregulated markets and the potential for economic catastrophe.

3. Exploitation of Labor

Capitalism has often been criticized for exploiting labor in the pursuit of profit. In the early industrial period, factory workers, including women and children, were subject to extremely harsh working conditions, long hours, and low wages. Though labor reforms have improved conditions in many developed countries, exploitation continues in various forms, particularly in developing nations where multinational corporations sometimes outsource labor to regions with lax labor laws. This "race to the bottom" mentality prioritizes profit over workers' rights and well-being, leading to modern-day sweatshops and child labor in some parts of the world.

4. Environmental Degradation

Another significant failure of capitalism is its contribution to environmental degradation. The pursuit of profit and economic growth often comes at the expense of natural resources and ecosystems. Industrial pollution, deforestation, overconsumption of fossil fuels, and mass production of waste have all been linked to capitalist practices. While capitalism has driven technological advancements, it has also fueled climate change, habitat destruction, and a growing ecological crisis. Critics argue that capitalism's focus on short-term profit undermines long-term sustainability, as industries prioritize cost-cutting over environmental protection.

5. Monopolies and Corporate Power

While capitalism promotes competition, it can also lead to monopolies and the concentration of corporate power. Large corporations, through mergers, acquisitions, and the sheer scale of their operations, can dominate markets, stifling competition and innovation. When a few large firms control significant portions of an industry, they can set prices, limit consumer choice, and exert undue influence over governments and regulatory bodies. Companies like Amazon, Google, and Facebook have faced criticism for monopolistic practices that limit competition and reduce market fairness.

6. Social Instability and Alienation

Capitalism can contribute to social instability by creating alienation between individuals and society. As individuals compete in capitalist systems, they can become isolated from their communities and disengaged from the social fabric. Economic inequality, lack of social mobility, and job insecurity can foster feelings of powerlessness and disillusionment, leading to increased mental health issues, social unrest, and political polarization. The "gig economy," for example, has created more flexible work opportunities, but it has also led to greater job insecurity and economic anxiety.

Conclusion

Capitalism has been both an engine of unprecedented economic growth and innovation, as well as a source of significant inequality, exploitation, and environmental harm. Its successes in raising standards of living, driving technological progress, and creating wealth are counterbalanced by its failures to address systemic inequality, prevent economic crises, and protect the environment. As we move forward, the challenge for capitalist economies is to find ways to mitigate these failures while preserving the dynamic and innovative spirit that has made capitalism a dominant force in the global economy. Social safety nets, environmental regulations, and wealth redistribution are some of the mechanisms that have been used to address the shortcomings of capitalism, but ongoing debates about the balance between market freedom and government intervention continue to shape the future of this economic system.

HISTORY OF MIXED ECONOMIES

A mixed economy is an economic system that combines elements of both capitalism and socialism, integrating private enterprise with government intervention to manage certain aspects of the economy. This balance allows free-market principles to coexist with policies aimed at addressing social inequalities and market failures. The concept emerged as a response to the extremes of laissez-faire capitalism and state-controlled socialism, seeking to harness the benefits of market efficiency while mitigating its most harmful effects through public oversight.

Early Development of Mixed Economies

The origins of mixed economies can be traced back to Europe in the 19th century, as governments responded to the social consequences of the Industrial Revolution. As capitalist economies rapidly industrialized, income inequality, poor working conditions, and lack of social protection led to calls for government intervention. Countries like Germany and the United Kingdom implemented social welfare policies, labor protections, and public health systems to balance the excesses of the free market. These reforms were some of the earliest steps toward what would later be recognized as mixed economic models.

Post-World War II Era

After World War II, mixed economies gained traction as nations sought to rebuild and stabilize their war-torn economies. Many Western countries, notably in Europe and North America, embraced a middle-ground approach, where capitalist markets operated alongside extensive government intervention in areas like healthcare, education, and social security. John Maynard Keynes' economic theories, which advocated for government intervention during economic downturns to stimulate demand and reduce unemployment, heavily influenced this shift. His ideas helped shape the modern welfare state, where governments regulate markets to ensure stability while providing social services to protect citizens from the vulnerabilities of capitalism.

Countries like the United Kingdom and Sweden expanded their welfare states and public services while still allowing private enterprise to flourish. This blending of capitalism and socialism laid the foundation for the mixed economies that dominate many developed nations today.

The Modern Era

Most modern developed nations, such as the United States, Canada, Germany, and Scandinavian countries, operate under some form of mixed economy. However, the degree of government intervention and the extent of social welfare systems vary widely. Over time, mixed economies have experienced waves of deregulation and privatization, particularly during the neoliberal era of the 1980s and 1990s. Yet, the basic structure of balancing market-driven growth with government oversight remains.

Successes of Mixed Economies

1. Economic Growth and Stability

Mixed economies are often successful in driving sustained economic growth while providing a degree of economic stability. The capitalist elements of mixed economies encourage entrepreneurship, innovation, and investment, contributing to technological advancement and industrial development. At the same time, government interventions, such as fiscal and monetary policies, can help prevent economic crises, smooth out business cycles, and mitigate the impacts of recessions. This stability allows for long-term growth and prosperity, as seen in countries like Germany, which combines a strong social safety net with a thriving industrial economy.

2. Social Welfare and Public Services

One of the key achievements of mixed economies is the provision of comprehensive social welfare systems. Governments in mixed economies ensure that citizens have access to basic needs like healthcare, education, and retirement benefits, which markets alone would not sufficiently provide. These systems reduce poverty, increase access to services, and enhance quality of life for many citizens. For example, Scandinavian countries such as Sweden and Norway offer universal healthcare, free education, and generous parental leave, resulting in relatively low poverty rates and high standards of living.

3. Balancing Market Efficiency with Social Equity

Mixed economies strike a balance between the efficiency of market competition and the government's role in addressing social inequalities. While private enterprises operate within the economy, governments in mixed economies intervene to correct market failures and redistribute wealth. This balance helps prevent extreme income inequality and ensures that a basic level of social protection is available to all. Countries like Canada have managed to maintain competitive economies while reducing inequality through progressive taxation, public healthcare, and income redistribution programs.

4. Flexibility in Economic Policy

Another success of mixed economies is their ability to adapt to changing economic conditions. Governments in mixed economies have the flexibility to adjust policies based on economic challenges, such as recessions, inflation, or unemployment. During economic downturns, they can increase public spending to stimulate growth or introduce welfare programs to cushion citizens against economic hardship. This flexibility helps mixed economies remain resilient and adaptable to both global market fluctuations and domestic crises.

Shortcomings of Mixed Economies

1. Focus on Financial Growth Over Individual Justice

While mixed economies are praised for balancing market growth with social protection, they often fail to create true individual justice. The primary focus of mixed economies tends to be on financial stability and economic growth rather than on ensuring comprehensive development and equality of opportunity for all individuals. In practice, mixed economies prioritize financial outcomes, such as GDP growth, over the holistic well-being and development of their citizens. The emphasis on financial performance can mask underlying inequalities in access to education, healthcare, social mobility, and cultural participation. As a result, individuals from marginalized communities often remain excluded from the full benefits of the economic system, even in countries with strong welfare states.

2. Inequality in Access to Opportunities

Although mixed economies implement policies to address income inequality, they often fail to ensure equality in access to opportunities for comprehensive development. Economic resources like education, healthcare, and social capital are distributed unevenly, leading to persistent gaps between the wealthy and the disadvantaged. For instance, in the U.S., a mixed economy with a robust private sector, access to quality education, healthcare, and job opportunities is heavily influenced by socio-economic status. This lack of equal access to opportunities exacerbates inequality, as those who start at a disadvantage find it difficult to break out of poverty, creating cycles of social exclusion.

3. Bureaucratic Inefficiency

Government involvement in the economy can sometimes lead to inefficiencies, particularly when public sector management becomes bloated or poorly coordinated. The allocation of resources through government programs may be less efficient than in competitive markets, leading to wasted resources, slow response times, or inadequate services. For example, public healthcare systems in some countries face long wait times and service delays due to bureaucratic complexities. In such cases, the inefficiency of government programs can undermine the very social protections they are designed to provide, limiting individuals' ability to access timely and effective services.

4. Market Inefficiencies and Overregulation

Mixed economies can suffer from market inefficiencies caused by excessive government regulation or intervention. Overregulation can stifle business innovation, increase operational costs, and create barriers to entry for new market players. When governments impose heavy regulations on industries, it can slow economic growth and reduce the competitiveness of businesses. In some mixed economies, government bailouts of failing industries or over-subsidization can distort markets and reward inefficient enterprises, leading to stagnant productivity.

5. Lack of Emphasis on Human Development

Mixed economies often neglect comprehensive human development, focusing instead on metrics like economic growth, unemployment rates, and inflation. In doing so, they may overlook key aspects of human development, such as emotional well-being, cultural participation, and personal growth. Governments in mixed economies may underinvest in areas that do not provide immediate financial returns, such as mental health services, arts and culture, or environmental sustainability. This lack of focus on holistic human development leaves many individuals feeling alienated or left behind in a system that prioritizes economic performance over personal fulfillment.

6. Continued Inequality Despite Redistribution Efforts

Even though mixed economies employ various methods of wealth redistribution, such as progressive taxation and social welfare programs, significant inequalities often persist. Redistribution mechanisms, while providing temporary relief, do not address the root causes of economic disparity, such as unequal access to education, health, and job opportunities. Moreover, wealthy individuals and corporations may exploit loopholes in the system to avoid taxes or minimize their contributions to the social welfare system. This weakens the effectiveness of redistribution efforts and leads to entrenched wealth disparities. Over time, the gap between the rich and the poor continues to widen, particularly in countries like the U.S. and U.K., where market forces dominate even within the framework of a mixed economy.

7. Inability to Address Long-Term Social Mobility

Another critical shortcoming of mixed economies is their inability to effectively promote long-term social mobility for disadvantaged groups. While social welfare programs may provide temporary support, they often do not lead to sustainable, generational change. Mixed economies tend to focus on short-term financial solutions rather than systemic reforms that promote long-term opportunity. For example, access to high-quality education, meaningful job training, and affordable healthcare are often limited for marginalized populations, leaving them trapped in cycles of poverty with little hope for upward mobility.

Mixed economies provide a pragmatic balance between the efficiencies of market systems and the social equity of government intervention, but they often fall short in ensuring individual justice and comprehensive human development. While successful in fostering economic stability, growth, and innovation, mixed economies still tend to focus on financial outcomes over social justice. The uneven distribution of opportunities for personal and comprehensive development, along with persistent income inequality, limits the potential of mixed economies to create truly inclusive societies. Governments in mixed economies must find ways to address these deeper inequalities and expand access to opportunities if they are to achieve a more just and equitable system that serves all citizens, not just the financially advantaged.

SHIFTING FROM PROFIT TO HUMAN DEVELOPMENT – REFRAMING SUCCESS IN THE NEW SOCIO-ECONOMIC SYSTEM

Introduction: The Existing Psychological Paradigm

In the current world, socio-economic systems have historically prioritized profit as the main driver of human activity. From the moment individuals enter society, they are taught to navigate a world where success is defined by material wealth, power, and external achievements. This prevailing paradigm influences how people perceive themselves, how they measure their accomplishments, and how they engage with the world around them.

The psychological impact of this profit-driven system is profound. It fosters an understanding of life that revolves around competition, acquisition, and external validation. Individuals are conditioned to believe that success is something to be obtained from external sources—whether through career advancements, financial gains, or social recognition. This has led to a societal structure where survival and success are intertwined with external competition, reinforcing the idea that personal worth is determined by one's ability to accumulate wealth, status, and material goods.

However, this approach creates a range of negative consequences: anxiety, burnout, dissatisfaction, and an unbalanced focus on individual achievement over communal well-being. The existing model of competition for profit perpetuates inequality, alienates individuals from their deeper personal development, and overlooks the need for internal fulfillment.

This chapter explores the need for a fundamental shift in socio-economic systems—a shift from an external, profit-driven model to one focused on human development, personal growth, and satisfaction. The aim is to redefine success and progress, moving from a society where individuals compete for external gains to one where they strive for internal growth, integration, and meaningful life experiences.

1. Profit as the Driver of Psychological Understanding

The dominant socio-economic systems in the modern world revolve around profit. Whether in capitalist or mixed economies, the pursuit of wealth and success has been the primary motivation for most individuals and organizations. As a result, the psychological understanding of success is almost entirely externally oriented. Society teaches individuals that their worth is measured by:

- **Financial success**: The accumulation of wealth becomes synonymous with personal achievement.
- **Social status**: Recognition from others, often tied to career milestones, becomes a marker of success.
- **Material gain**: Possessing more assets and resources is viewed as the pinnacle of accomplishment.

This has created a culture of competition, where individuals are pitted against one another in a constant race for limited resources. The individual is expected to achieve success by out-competing others, whether in the workplace, the marketplace, or the social arena. This relentless focus on external achievement leads to a fragmented sense of self, where people measure their worth by how they compare to others rather than by their internal growth or fulfillment.

The problem with this approach is that it alienates individuals from their internal development. The human mind, when conditioned to view success solely in external terms, becomes disconnected from its deeper needs for emotional integration, purpose, and satisfaction. As a result, many people, even those who achieve great wealth or social status, often feel unfulfilled, anxious, or dissatisfied.

2. The Need for a New Psychological Approach to Success

One of the main objectives of the proposed system is to transform this psychological understanding of success. The focus shifts from external validation and profit to a model where success is defined by internal growth, personal development, and integration. This new system reorients individuals away from the idea that life is a competition for external rewards and toward the understanding that life is a journey of internal discovery and self-improvement.

Key elements of this new psychological approach include:

- **Personal Fulfillment as the Core of Success**: Success is no longer measured by how much an individual has gained in the material world but by how much they have grown in terms of self-awareness, emotional well-being, and personal satisfaction.
- **Integration of the Self**: Individuals are encouraged to seek harmony within themselves—balancing their intellectual, emotional, and physical needs. This creates a more holistic understanding of personal achievement, where growth is defined by internal coherence rather than external benchmarks.
- **Redefining Competition**: In this new system, competition is internalized. Instead of competing with others, individuals are encouraged to compete with their previous selves, striving to improve, learn, and grow continuously. This transforms the dynamic from one of external conflict to one of internal development.

This psychological shift is crucial for the long-term success of the socio-economic system. It encourages people to focus on self-improvement rather than endless accumulation, helping to alleviate the stress, anxiety, and dissatisfaction that arise from constant external competition.

3. Human Development as the New Socio-Economic Driver

In the new socio-economic system, the primary focus is not profit, but human development. This means that the success of the system is measured not by economic growth or material wealth, but by the development of individuals—emotionally, intellectually, and socially.

This change in focus alters the way society functions at every level:

- **Education Systems**: The education system is redesigned to prioritize personal development, critical thinking, and emotional intelligence over training for profit-driven careers. Individuals are encouraged to pursue knowledge and skills that foster their personal growth rather than simply preparing them for economic productivity.
- **Work and Employment**: The workplace is no longer a place for relentless competition but a space for collaborative growth. Employees are rewarded not for their ability to out-compete others but for their contributions to the development of themselves and their colleagues. This creates a culture of mutual support rather than individual competition.
- **Social Structures**: The system encourages integration and community building, where individuals contribute to society not through accumulation but through nurturing relationships and supporting the growth of others. This creates a sense of belonging and shared responsibility for collective well-being.

By shifting the socio-economic focus from profit to human development, individuals are no longer seen as tools for economic productivity. Instead, they are viewed as complex, evolving beings whose primary goal is to grow and develop in all aspects of their lives.

4. Redefining Success: From External Acquisition to Internal Growth

One of the most profound changes in the proposed system is the redefinition of success. In the current model, success is often equated with how much an individual can accumulate or gain from external sources—money, power, influence. The new system shifts this focus inward.

Success is redefined by:

- **Personal Integration**: Success means achieving a sense of wholeness and coherence within oneself. Individuals are encouraged to explore their own potential, work on their weaknesses, and find balance between different aspects of their lives.
- **Satisfaction and Well-Being**: Success is measured by one's level of personal satisfaction and emotional well-being. Instead of seeking external rewards, individuals pursue activities, relationships, and experiences that fulfill their deeper psychological needs.
- **Contribution to Human Development**: Success is not only about personal growth but about contributing to the growth and development of others. This means that individuals are recognized and rewarded not for how

much they can gain but for how much they can help others grow.

This redefinition of success encourages a paradigm shift in how people view their role in society. Instead of striving to out-compete others, individuals are empowered to focus on internal development and cooperative growth. This creates a more harmonious society where personal satisfaction and collective well-being are intertwined.

5. The Systemic Impact of Changing the Psychological Approach

Changing the psychological approach to life and success from external competition to internal development has far-reaching implications for the socio-economic system:

- **Reduced Inequality**: The focus on personal growth and satisfaction reduces the pressure to accumulate wealth, which in turn helps minimize economic disparity. The system no longer glorifies the wealthy but honors those who contribute to human development and personal fulfillment.
- **Increased Well-Being**: As individuals shift their focus from external acquisition to internal growth, levels of stress, anxiety, and burnout are reduced. People are no longer trapped in the rat race of endless competition but are free to pursue lives of meaning and satisfaction.
- **Sustainable Societal Progress**: The system becomes more sustainable as it is no longer driven by relentless consumption and profit. Human development, rather than economic expansion, becomes the engine of

societal progress, creating a system that fosters long-term stability and well-being.

Toward a New Understanding of Life and Success

The transition from a profit-driven socio-economic system to one centered on human development represents a revolutionary shift in how individuals understand life and success. In this new paradigm, success is no longer an external competition for survival, but an internal journey toward personal integration, fulfillment, and satisfaction. By changing the psychological approach to life, the system empowers individuals to lead more meaningful lives while contributing to the collective development of society.

This chapter outlines the need for such a transformation and how the proposed system facilitates this shift. It calls for a reimagining of societal values, where human growth and personal well-being replace profit as the primary measure of success.

BUILDING A SYSTEM ON SOLID FOUNDATION

To create a socio-economic system that balances profit with fulfillment and progress, it's essential to understand human psychological needs and drives. A system that only focuses on material wealth will neglect key aspects of human motivation, such as purpose, social connection, and personal growth. To address this, the following considerations should be made:

- **Self-Determination Theory (SDT):** This psychological theory emphasizes the importance of three core needs

—autonomy, competence, and relatedness. The system should create opportunities for individuals to experience:

- **Autonomy:** Giving people control over their own lives, economic choices, and contributions.
- **Competence:** Ensuring opportunities for individuals to develop skills and experience success, both personally and professionally.
- **Relatedness:** Building community and social connections, as fulfilling relationships are a cornerstone of psychological well-being.

- **Mixing Profit with Purpose:** Encourage businesses and individuals to seek purpose alongside profit. Companies can integrate social responsibility and positive impact into their missions, motivating workers and entrepreneurs to feel that their work contributes meaningfully to society, in addition to financial success.

- **Recognition of Non-Monetary Value:** Acknowledging that human fulfillment goes beyond material wealth, the system should value work that contributes to emotional well-being, creativity, and social impact. This includes rewarding work in caregiving, arts, community building, and mental health support.

1. Individual Ownership and Sense of Accomplishment

Ownership and personal accomplishment are fundamental to psychological well-being. A successful socio-economic system should create a balance between individual ownership and social equity, allowing people to pursue personal goals while minimizing the inequality that arises from unchecked capitalism.

- **Distributed Ownership Models:** Encourage systems of distributed or cooperative ownership, where individuals have a stake in the success of their enterprises without exacerbating wealth inequality. Cooperative models allow workers to share profits and decision-making power, ensuring that success is broadly shared rather than concentrated among a few.
- **Supporting Entrepreneurship:** The system should encourage entrepreneurship by providing access to education, resources, and support for individuals to start their own businesses. At the same time, it should ensure that entrepreneurs operate within a framework that discourages exploitative practices or excessive concentration of wealth.
- **Rewarding Contributions Beyond Profit:** Individuals should feel a sense of accomplishment not only for financial success but for meaningful contributions to their communities and society. Recognizing and rewarding efforts in education, social work, environmental sustainability, and innovation can foster a culture of personal achievement while benefiting the broader system.

2. Minimizing Disparity and Promoting Equity

To minimize economic disparity, the socio-economic system should be designed to distribute resources and opportunities more fairly while still allowing individuals to pursue success. Key components include:

- **Universal Basic Services:** Guarantee access to essential services, such as healthcare, education, housing, and transportation, to ensure that all individuals have a fair starting point. Access to these services can help reduce poverty and disparity while enabling individuals to focus on personal and professional fulfillment.
- **Living Wages and Fair Labor Practices:** Establish living wage standards to ensure that everyone can meet their basic needs through work, reducing income inequality. This should be paired with strong labor protections to prevent exploitation and ensure that workers are treated fairly, with rights to safe working conditions and opportunities for advancement.
- **Wealth-Building Opportunities for All:** Create systems that allow all individuals to build wealth over time, such as through affordable housing programs, employee stock ownership plans (ESOPs), and accessible retirement savings programs. These systems can help ensure that people from all backgrounds have opportunities for financial security and upward mobility.

3. Building a System of Service and Facilitation

A core principle of this socio-economic system should be that the system exists to serve the individual, rather than the individual being a tool for the system. This principle ensures that human welfare and individual fulfillment are prioritized over profit and growth for their own sake.

- **Government and Institutions as Facilitators:** Instead of controlling economic activity, governments and institutions should act as facilitators, ensuring that individuals have access to the resources and infrastructure they need to succeed. This includes creating regulatory frameworks that encourage innovation, protect workers, and promote social welfare, while leaving space for individual initiative and freedom.
- **Human-Centered Policy Design:** Policies should be designed with a focus on improving human well-being, not just economic indicators like GDP. For example, policies that encourage work-life balance, mental health support, and community involvement can create a more holistic and humane society.
- **Decentralized Decision-Making:** Empower communities to make decisions that affect their own well-being and economic development. Decentralized governance can allow for more localized solutions that better reflect the needs and desires of the people they serve, promoting a sense of ownership and involvement in the system.
- **Public Institutions Focused on Personal Development:** Rather than merely focusing on economic efficiency, public institutions should also prioritize personal development and fulfillment. This could include lifelong learning programs, mental health support systems, and platforms for creative and

community-building activities.

4. Sustainability and Long-Term Thinking

A sustainable socio-economic system should focus on long-term well-being rather than short-term financial gain. This includes both environmental sustainability and the sustainable development of human potential.

- **Green Economy Focus:** Transitioning to a green economy, where economic activity is aligned with environmental sustainability, ensures that the system promotes not only human well-being but also the well-being of future generations. Incentivizing sustainable business practices, such as renewable energy, conservation, and circular economies, helps balance profit with ecological responsibility.
- **Long-Term Investment in Human Capital:** A successful system should invest in education, skills training, and personal development over the long term. Rather than treating individuals as temporary labor, the system should view them as assets to be cultivated and supported throughout their lives, ensuring that they can continue to contribute to society while achieving personal growth and fulfillment.

Conclusion

Building a socio-economic system that integrates psychological fulfillment, individual ownership, and equity requires a comprehensive approach that balances the needs for financial progress, personal fulfillment, and social justice. By focusing on holistic human development, ensuring broad access to opportunities, and structuring institutions to serve individuals rather than exploiting them, such a system can foster a more equitable and fulfilling society. This approach not only ensures personal accomplishment but also minimizes disparity and promotes a more humane, purpose-driven economy.

PROPOSED SOCIO-ECONOMIC MODEL

In this proposed economic model, wealth distribution is addressed through balanced ownership structures that distribute the profits and decision-making power across three key stakeholders: the government, entrepreneurs, and employees. This model encourages shared responsibility and benefits, aligning the interests of various stakeholders while promoting fair wealth distribution.

Key Aspects of the Ownership Structure:

1. Government-Funded Businesses:

- **40% Government Ownership:** The government, as a funding entity, retains significant ownership, ensuring that public resources are invested with a return that benefits society. The government's role here is not only as a regulator but as an active participant in the economic system, ensuring public oversight, stability, and reinvestment in social welfare and infrastructure.
- **35% Entrepreneur Ownership:** The entrepreneur, who contributes expertise, vision, and leadership, holds a substantial share of the business. This incentivizes innovation and entrepreneurial activity, allowing

individuals to benefit directly from the success of the businesses they create.

- **25% Employee Ownership:** Employees hold a significant ownership stake, ensuring that those who contribute their labor and skills are directly involved in decision-making and benefit from the success of the business. This encourages employee loyalty, productivity, and a sense of ownership over the company's future.

2. Entrepreneur-Funded Businesses:

- **25% Government Ownership:** Even in businesses funded by entrepreneurs, the government retains a portion of ownership. This allows for public accountability and ensures that the broader society benefits from economic growth. The government's ownership share can also be used to fund social programs or reinvest in public goods.
- **45% Entrepreneur Ownership:** Entrepreneurs, who take on the most significant financial risks, maintain the largest ownership stake. This rewards risk-taking, innovation, and investment, driving economic activity and new business creation.
- **30% Employee Ownership:** Employees in these businesses have a larger share than in government-funded businesses, reflecting the critical role they play in contributing to the success of the business. By giving employees a direct financial stake, this model promotes wealth distribution, improves workplace morale, and enhances long-term commitment to the company's

goals.

Benefits of This Ownership Structure:

- **Fair Wealth Distribution:** By distributing ownership among the government, entrepreneurs, and employees, the model ensures that profits and wealth are more evenly spread. Entrepreneurs are still rewarded for innovation and risk-taking, while employees share in the financial success of the businesses they help build.
- **Employee Empowerment:** Employee ownership gives workers a voice in decision-making and an incentive to see the business succeed. This can lead to higher productivity, greater job satisfaction, and a sense of shared purpose.
- **Government Accountability:** Government ownership ensures that public investments in businesses yield returns that can be used to benefit the broader society. It also allows the government to have a say in corporate governance, promoting ethical practices and sustainable business models.
- **Entrepreneurial Incentives:** The model still provides significant incentives for entrepreneurs to create and grow businesses, as they retain a substantial ownership share. This ensures that the economy remains dynamic and innovative, while also fostering collaboration between private and public sectors.

Challenges and Considerations:

- **Balancing Stakeholder Interests:** Ensuring that the interests of the government, entrepreneurs, and employees align may require careful governance structures. Decision-making mechanisms will need to be in place to prevent conflicts and ensure that the business operates efficiently.
- **Government's Role in the Economy:** This model assumes an active role for the government in business ownership, which may be more suitable for certain economic contexts than others. The government will need to balance its dual roles as a regulator and an owner.
- **Entrepreneurial Risk:** In entrepreneur-funded businesses, entrepreneurs take on a larger financial risk. While they are rewarded with a significant ownership share, mechanisms should be in place to ensure that entrepreneurs are adequately supported during periods of financial hardship or market downturns.

Conclusion

In designing an economic model that promotes fair wealth distribution, balanced ownership structures offer a transformative approach to achieving a more equitable society. By distributing ownership among the government, entrepreneurs, and employees, this model fosters a sense of shared responsibility and mutual benefit, aligning the interests of all key stakeholders. It ensures that while entrepreneurs are incentivized for their risk-taking and innovation, employees also share in the success of the businesses they help build, creating a more inclusive economy.

The integration of the government as an active participant in business ownership not only ensures public accountability and ethical governance but also provides a mechanism to reinvest wealth into society, supporting public services, infrastructure, and social welfare programs. This dual role enhances the overall stability of the system, protecting it from the excesses and failures of pure market-driven capitalism.

Yet, as promising as this approach may be, the challenge lies in maintaining the delicate balance between these different stakeholders. Careful governance and decision-making processes will be critical to ensuring that all parties can coexist harmoniously and work toward common goals. Moreover, the model must remain flexible enough to adapt to the changing needs of the economy and the individuals it serves.

Ultimately, this model represents a shift toward a more human-centered economic system—one that not only encourages innovation and financial progress but also prioritizes the well-being and fulfillment of individuals. By combining the strengths of entrepreneurial ambition with a commitment to social equity, this economic model can pave the way for a future where prosperity is shared more fairly, and economic systems truly serve the people they were designed to support.

As we move forward, the success of such a system will depend on our collective ability to refine its principles, overcome challenges, and remain focused on creating an economy that serves both the individual and society. With thoughtful implementation, this model has the potential to not only minimize disparity but to redefine the very purpose of economic progress—moving beyond profit to include fulfillment, sustainability, and long-term human development.

SOCIO-ECONOMICALLY AND ECOLOGICALLY SPEAKING

In order for humanity to evolve, we must become the point of interaction between ecology and technology, working to sustain and merge them into a symbiotic relationship that respects both. This requires a balance where technological advancements do not come at the expense of ecological health, but instead, both systems are integrated to enhance each other. Technology must be developed with an awareness of its environmental impact, while ecology must be seen as a crucial factor in guiding technological progress. Only through this harmonious interaction can we ensure sustainable growth and long-term survival.

By creating a symbiotic relationship between ecology and technology, we not only protect natural ecosystems but also drive innovation in ways that promote environmental resilience. This approach demands that we rethink our current technological practices to align with ecological principles, ensuring that our advancements contribute to the restoration and preservation of the environment. Through this merger, we can create a future where both technological progress and ecological health coexist, driving human development in a way that respects the planet's natural systems and secures the well-being of future generations.

Even our modern approach to eco-friendliness is influenced by capitalist frameworks, which limits its overall efficiency. Efforts to promote sustainability are often driven by market forces, where eco-friendly products and solutions become commodities for profit. This creates a system where access to sustainable alternatives is tied to consumer spending power, leaving lower-income groups unable to fully participate in environmentally responsible practices. As a result, the socio-economic divide hinders the broader adoption of sustainable solutions, preventing society from achieving true ecological balance.

The socio-economic part-nature of the problem means that environmental initiatives often prioritize profitability over accessibility and long-term impact. While green technologies and eco-friendly products may provide some benefit, their reach remains limited to those who can afford them, creating a superficial layer of environmentalism. To address the environmental crisis effectively, it is necessary to challenge the socio-economic barriers that restrict access to sustainable living. This requires a shift from treating eco-friendliness as a market-driven trend to a fundamental societal responsibility, ensuring that sustainable practices are available and achievable for everyone, regardless of economic status.

Even at its core, the modern approach to eco-friendliness often relies on the rapid extraction of minerals, revealing capitalist interests beneath the surface. The push for green technologies like electric vehicles, solar panels, and batteries requires significant amounts of rare earth minerals and other resources. This demand drives a cycle of accelerated extraction, often at the expense of environmental health and vulnerable communities. While marketed as solutions to environmental problems, these technologies are frequently tied to profit-driven agendas, prioritizing short-term gains over sustainable resource management.

The focus on resource-intensive technologies perpetuates a system that still operates within the framework of consumption and profit maximization. The capitalist approach, focused on faster extraction and commodification of natural resources, undermines the long-term goal of true sustainability. By pursuing eco-friendly solutions through a lens of economic gain, the environmental movement risks reinforcing the very problems it aims to solve, making it crucial to reconsider how we approach sustainability. A shift towards slower, more responsible resource use, integrated with broader socio-economic reforms, is needed to break free from this cycle.

The main reason for the inefficiency in capitalistic approaches to eco-friendliness is that profitability takes precedence over sustainability and long-term ecological health. In capitalist systems, economic gain is prioritized, driving companies and industries to focus on short-term profits rather than the long-term environmental impact of their actions. As a result, even green technologies and eco-friendly initiatives are often developed and marketed with the primary goal of generating profit, rather than creating truly sustainable solutions. This emphasis on profitability leads to practices like faster extraction of natural resources, which undermines the overall objective of preserving the environment.

Because profitability remains the top priority, sustainable practices are often compromised or limited to what can be commodified and sold. Long-term ecological concerns are sidelined, as the economic model revolves around continuous consumption and growth. This short-term thinking prevents society from fully committing to the deep, structural changes required for genuine sustainability, such as reducing resource consumption or investing in technologies that may not yield immediate financial returns but are essential for the future. Without reorienting the focus from profit to long-term ecological balance, true sustainability will remain difficult to achieve in a capitalist framework.

This is where the concept of a symbiotic relationship between ecology and technology comes into play. Rather than prioritizing short-term profitability, this approach seeks to balance economic growth with environmental sustainability. In a true symbiotic relationship, technological advancements would be designed not for quick financial gain but to work in harmony with ecological systems, ensuring long-term benefits for both society and the environment. By integrating ecology and technology in this way, the emphasis shifts from extraction and consumption to preservation and regeneration.

This symbiotic relationship would redefine the way we view progress, moving beyond the profit-driven motives of capitalist systems. Instead, the focus would be on creating systems that not only drive innovation but also ensure the health and stability of the planet's ecosystems. Technologies would be developed with sustainability as a core principle, promoting resource efficiency, circular economies, and renewable energy sources that minimize environmental harm. By fostering this balance, we can create a future where economic growth and ecological preservation coexist, ensuring both human prosperity and the planet's well-being.

Conclusion

Addressing the shortcomings of our current eco-friendly approaches requires a fundamental shift in priorities, moving away from short-term profit and toward a deeper focus on sustainability. The capitalist-driven push for faster resource extraction, even in the name of green technology, highlights the core issue—profitability remains the top concern. This model limits the effectiveness of environmental solutions and perpetuates the same cycles of exploitation and imbalance. True sustainability cannot be achieved through surface-level fixes or commodification but must come from restructuring how we engage with both technology and the environment.

The solution lies in creating a relationship between ecology and technology, where both systems support and sustain each other in a way that respects long-term ecological health. By realigning technological advancements with environmental preservation and shifting away from the profit-first mindset, we can ensure that human progress and the health of the planet coexist. This requires rethinking not only economic structures but also societal values, prioritizing sustainability as a core driver of innovation and growth. Only through this balanced integration can we address the root causes of inequality, ecological degradation, and create a truly sustainable future.

GOVERNANCE

HISTORICAL DEVELOPMENT OF DEMOCRACY AND ITS ROOTS IN GROUP MENTALITY

The concept of democracy, often hailed as one of the most significant advancements in human governance, traces its roots back to ancient forms of collective decision-making within small communities, families, and tribes. Before democracy became institutionalized, it emerged organically from the group dynamics that governed early human societies. Understanding this foundation is crucial to appreciating the system's development and its potential flaws.

Early Group Decision-Making: The Family and Tribe

In pre-modern human societies, the family unit was the core of both survival and organization. The family, an extension of larger kinship groups, represented the earliest form of governance, where decisions were made collectively or by a designated elder, who often represented the wisdom and experience of the group. These early structures reflected a proto-democratic ideal, as each member's survival and well-being were tied to the collective, thus ensuring that decisions had to account for the group's best interests.

In hunter-gatherer societies, tribal groups would often convene councils of elders or rely on collective deliberation to make decisions about hunting, conflict resolution, and resource distribution. The tribe's survival hinged on cooperation and shared responsibilities, and these early group-based systems created the foundation for democratic principles like shared governance and accountability. Leaders in these settings were often chosen based on merit—skills in leadership, hunting, or diplomacy—an early form of democratic selection rooted in meritocracy.

The Birth of City-States and Formal Democracy

As human societies transitioned from nomadic lifestyles to more settled agricultural communities, the need for formal governance structures grew. Ancient city-states, such as those in Mesopotamia and Egypt, initially relied on monarchs or religious figures to govern. However, the first formalized systems of democracy emerged in ancient Greece, particularly in Athens around the 5th century BCE.

The development of Athenian democracy was a significant leap forward in governance. For the first time, citizens (though restricted to free male citizens, excluding women, slaves, and foreigners) were given the right to participate in decision-making processes, establishing the foundations of democratic governance as a formal system. This Athenian model of direct democracy allowed citizens to debate and vote on laws, military campaigns, and civic decisions, demonstrating the power of collective input. The famous *Ekklesia* (assembly) and *Boule* (council) were the main institutions that enabled citizens to have a voice in governance, promoting shared responsibility for the well-being of the state.

The concept of democracy in Athens was deeply rooted in the idea that the collective was greater than the individual, a notion inherited from earlier group mentalities within family and tribal structures. Decisions made by the majority were considered to represent the wisdom of the populace, with the belief that governance was best served by consulting the many rather than leaving it to a select few. However, the Athenian system also revealed the vulnerabilities of direct democracy, particularly its susceptibility to populism and short-term thinking, issues that will be explored later in this chapter.

Roman Republic: Representation and Merit

While Athens pioneered direct democracy, the Roman Republic, established in 509 BCE, introduced a different model —representative democracy. In Rome, citizens elected representatives, known as senators, to make decisions on their behalf, a system designed to maintain order in a larger and more complex society. This representative system recognized that not every citizen had the time, knowledge, or resources to participate directly in governance, yet it preserved the idea that the people should have a voice in selecting their leaders.

The Roman system also incorporated meritocratic elements. Senators were often chosen based on their achievements in military service, diplomacy, or economic success, reflecting the idea that those with proven capabilities should guide the republic. This blend of representation and meritocracy is a precursor to modern democratic systems and serves as an important historical example of how democracy can be balanced with competence-based leadership.

The Roman model was far from perfect, with power often concentrated among elites, but it established the foundations for later democratic institutions, including modern parliamentary systems. The tension between direct democracy, as seen in Athens, and representative democracy, as demonstrated in Rome, would become a central theme in the evolution of governance over the centuries.

Medieval and Early Modern Developments

During the medieval period, democracy receded as feudalism and monarchies dominated Europe. However, forms of proto-democratic governance survived in local councils, guilds, and town meetings, where community members had some say in local decisions. These small-scale participatory structures kept the democratic spirit alive at the grassroots level, even as monarchies wielded centralized power.

The modern era saw the revival and transformation of democratic ideas, particularly during the Enlightenment, which laid the philosophical groundwork for modern democracy. Thinkers such as John Locke, Jean-Jacques Rousseau, and Montesquieu expanded on the idea that governance should be derived from the consent of the governed. These philosophers argued that individual rights, equality, and freedom were paramount, thus shaping the democratic revolutions of the late 18th century, such as the American and French revolutions.

Democracy in Modern Times: From Local to Global

The modern version of democracy, built on these historical foundations, reflects the tension between group mentality and individual rights. Today, democracy is a global phenomenon, but it often manifests in diverse forms—liberal democracies, social democracies, and hybrid systems. The common thread through all these forms of democracy is the idea that governance should reflect the will of the people, just as early human societies organized around collective decision-making.

At its core, democracy continues to be about balancing the needs and interests of the group with the autonomy and rights of individuals. The legacy of family and tribal decision-making structures still lingers in democratic principles today, as nations grapple with how to create systems that serve both the collective good and individual fulfillment.

The Core Issues With Group Mentality Dynamics

The core issue with group mentality is the inherent asymmetry in awareness and consideration between the individual and the group. Individuals are often well aware of the group's needs and are conditioned to prioritize them, contributing to the well-being of the collective. However, the group is not necessarily designed to recognize or address the nuanced needs of each individual. The foundational principle of group dynamics tends to prioritize the benefit of the whole over the individual, which leads to situations where individuals' needs are overlooked or sacrificed. This creates an imbalance where the group expects loyalty and contribution from its members, but it doesn't always reciprocate with the same level of care for each individual's well-being.

Not only is there an asymmetry in recognizing individual needs, but the group itself transforms into a collective entity, and individual needs are often subsumed into collective needs. As the group becomes more psychologically cohesive around the collective, the distinction between individuals blurs, and the focus shifts almost entirely to what benefits the collective. Individual needs are no longer seen as unique, but rather as components that must align with the collective agenda. This collective mentality tends to standardize needs, erasing the diversity of personal experiences, which can lead to the suppression of individuality in favor of the perceived good of the whole. The individual is expected to align with and support these collective needs, often at the cost of their own, which creates a dynamic where the group expects conformity while the individual's unique needs are sidelined.

Additionally, many problems that individuals face are often accompanied by a sense of shame or societal taboo, which can threaten their social standing and discourage them from seeking help. These personal challenges, which may include mental health issues, financial struggles, or personal failures, carry a stigma that makes individuals hesitant to express their needs openly within the group. On the other hand, group needs tend to be more broadly acknowledged and free of stigma, creating a situation where collective concerns are easier to address, while individuals suffer in silence. This dynamic further reinforces the imbalance where the group's needs are prioritized and supported, whereas the individual's struggles remain hidden, often without adequate support or understanding.

It is the group itself that establishes the taboos and norms, often creating the conditions that make certain individual struggles feel shameful or unacceptable. These taboos are formed to maintain the cohesion and perceived strength of the collective, discouraging behaviors or issues that are viewed as threats to group stability. As a result, individuals facing such challenges are pressured to conform or hide their struggles to avoid judgment, exclusion, or loss of standing. This creates a cycle where the group, in its effort to protect collective values, suppresses individual vulnerabilities, making it even harder for members to seek help or express their authentic needs. Thus, the collective's interest in maintaining its image can end up marginalizing those within it, ultimately prioritizing conformity over genuine support for its members.

Not only does the group establish taboos and suppress individual needs, but it also tends to cultivate members who fully identify with the collective, blurring the line between the individual and the group within their own identity. This identification becomes so strong that individuals internalize the group's values, norms, and goals as their own, often without question. This process prevents the development of true individualization, where a person forms their own distinct values and sense of self, independent of group influence. As individuals increasingly merge their identities with the collective, they lose the ability to recognize and prioritize their unique needs, desires, and perspectives, effectively becoming extensions of the group rather than autonomous beings. This loss of self makes it difficult to challenge group norms or seek help for personal struggles that fall outside of collective acceptance, reinforcing a cycle of conformity and dependency on the group.

When individuals fully merge their identities with the group, it puts them at significant risk if the group disperses or disintegrates. If the group falls apart—due to social, political, or organizational changes—individuals who have deeply identified with it may find themselves lost, lacking a sense of identity, purpose, or direction. The collapse of the collective can leave them without the support structures, roles, or values that once defined their existence, creating an identity crisis. Their reliance on the group for validation and meaning makes it difficult for them to adapt and find a new path independently, leaving them vulnerable and disoriented in the absence of the collective framework they depended on. This underscores the potential dangers of over-identification with a group, where individual autonomy and self-definition are sacrificed, leaving the person without an anchor when the group can no longer provide stability.

Another point is that groups often form in response to perceived threats, whether real or imagined, and in doing so, they often end up reinforcing or even creating the existence of that threat in a more substantial form. The collective identity is frequently built around the notion of overcoming or opposing a common enemy, which can lead to the threat being magnified in importance, as it becomes a core part of the group's purpose and cohesion. This dynamic can perpetuate a cycle where the group's existence and unity depend on the ongoing perception of the threat, thereby keeping the threat alive, regardless of whether it is still valid or has been exaggerated. It's a feedback loop where the collective's identity, fear, and response continually validate the threat, giving it a form of permanence and power that it might not otherwise have had. This phenomenon can limit the group's evolution and prevent individuals from seeing beyond the perceived threat, stifling growth and exploration of other potential paths or solutions.

The fundamental nature of group ideology often limits its capacity to perceive its position within a broader context. Groups tend to adopt rigid beliefs and narratives that define their identity, which prevents them from recognizing the changing realities and evolving dynamics beyond their immediate scope. This lack of adaptability leads to a self-reinforcing cycle where the group interprets any change in the broader context as a continuation of oppression or an external threat, rather than an opportunity for transformation or growth.

By narrowing its focus to uphold its core ideology, the group is inclined to overlook how it may be out of sync with the larger environment. Instead of adapting or reconsidering its beliefs, the group often doubles down on its sense of being oppressed or under threat, which serves to further unite its members and justify its actions. This narrative of ongoing struggle becomes essential to maintaining group cohesion, even when it may no longer accurately reflect reality.

Ultimately, this inability to contextualize itself within broader changes prevents the group from evolving and engaging constructively with external developments, thereby perpetuating an insular and potentially self-defeating cycle. The group's ideology becomes a barrier, keeping it from seeing how its goals and values might need to change or expand in response to the wider world. This dynamic reinforces a sense of victimhood and limits any true progress toward resilience and transformation.

This highlights the need for a system that fosters independent identities while still being rooted in shared values capable of enduring the uncertainties of life. Such a system would encourage individuals to develop their unique sense of self, cultivating personal autonomy and resilience, while also maintaining a connection to common principles that bind people together in times of need. By balancing personal growth with a sense of community, this approach would help individuals navigate challenges both independently and collectively, without losing their individuality. It would allow people to benefit from the support of a group while retaining their personal identity, ensuring that if the group disperses or undergoes changes, they still have a strong foundation upon which to build their lives. This would create a more adaptive, resilient society where both the individual and the collective can coexist in harmony, each capable of thriving even in the face of uncertainty.

EFFECTS OF AN INDIVIDUALISTIC SYSTEM ON INFORMATIONAL INTERACTION

The issue with modern group dynamics is that they inherently amplify echo chambers and facilitate the spread of misinformation, primarily by conditioning individuals to rely on collective reinforcement rather than independent, critical thinking. In our increasingly interconnected world, people often base their beliefs on what aligns with their chosen group's ideology, reducing the drive to seek out, or even consider, alternative perspectives. These group-based validations shape not only what is accepted as true but also how aggressively dissenting opinions are dismissed. When people rely on collective thinking to this extent, the very structure of society shifts to prioritize cohesion over truth, and this dynamic severely limits critical thought at an individual level, undermining the capacity for people to evaluate information independently and question prevailing narratives.

A society rooted in individualism, by contrast, would promote a culture where individuals are encouraged—and expected—to form their own beliefs based on personal reasoning rather than group consensus. This kind of societal structure places emphasis on self-reflection, skepticism, and intellectual independence, which naturally fosters a more critical populace. In an individualistic model, people would be less likely to accept information simply because it aligns with a familiar narrative; instead, they would analyze information in light of their understanding, aiming to uncover truth rather than conform to group expectations. By prioritizing the individual's role in knowledge formation, this structure would empower people to actively dismantle echo chambers and scrutinize the validity of information before accepting it, resulting in a society where truth-seeking becomes more central than conformity.

Moreover, education in an individualistic society would focus less on social compliance and more on cultivating analytical skills and intellectual resilience. The education system would prioritize developing students' abilities to think critically, question assumptions, and analyze ideas deeply and independently. This approach goes beyond simply delivering knowledge; it seeks to empower individuals to understand, apply, and challenge information autonomously. When education fosters self-sufficient thinkers, society benefits as a whole, as individuals are better equipped to detect misinformation, reject superficial explanations, and make decisions based on nuanced understanding rather than group-aligned beliefs. This shift in educational focus would create a social base that is not only informed but capable of questioning and evolving beyond simplistic narratives or unsubstantiated claims.

An individualistic societal model would also shift the nature of public discourse, making it less about echoing pre-approved ideas and more about fostering genuine, critical debate. Today's group dynamics often prioritize cohesion, creating environments where conflicting perspectives are stifled or marginalized to maintain unity. In contrast, an individualistic model would encourage open dialogue and critical engagement, where people are free to disagree and challenge each other in the pursuit of truth. This openness would disrupt echo chambers by introducing diverse perspectives, allowing truth to emerge through the dialectical process rather than as a reflection of group loyalty. In such an environment, misinformation would have a harder time taking root, as it would face continual scrutiny and debate rather than passive acceptance.

Ultimately, the core issue with current group dynamics is that they prioritize cohesion over intellectual independence, leading to a society where echo chambers thrive and misinformation spreads easily. By shifting toward individualism, society could dismantle these echo chambers, creating a culture that values critical thought, intellectual independence, and open discourse. An individualistic model would promote a truth-oriented society, where individuals are encouraged to think for themselves, question everything, and engage in genuine dialogue. This foundational shift would make it more difficult for misinformation to persist, fostering a culture of inquiry rather than conformity and equipping individuals to navigate the complexities of modern information landscapes with resilience and insight.

THE PROBLEM WITH VOLATILITY IN PURE DEMOCRACY AND THE POPULAR APPROACH ON NATIONAL AND INTERNATIONAL TRADE AND POLITICS

While democracy is celebrated for granting individuals the right to participate in governance, pure democracy—where decisions are made directly by the majority—often leads to significant volatility, particularly in areas like national and international trade and politics. This volatility arises because democratic systems, when driven purely by popular opinion, are inherently unstable and susceptible to short-term thinking, populism, and emotional decision-making. In the context of global trade and politics, such instability can create uncertainty, disrupt long-term strategic planning, and hinder the capacity to form reliable and sustainable partnerships.

1. The Short-Term Nature of Popular Decisions

In purely democratic systems, the majority opinion often dictates the outcome of critical decisions. While this embodies the principle of popular sovereignty, it also exposes a core weakness: the tendency to prioritize short-term gains over long-term stability. In many cases, the public's immediate concerns—such as unemployment, inflation, or a desire for rapid reform—may drive policies that neglect the broader, long-term consequences for the economy, society, or international relations.

For instance, decisions around national trade policies can be heavily influenced by temporary economic pressures or political promises made to secure votes. If a majority of the population feels that a particular trade agreement is unfavorable, a purely democratic process may overturn or renegotiate deals that took years to construct, even if the long-term benefits are substantial. This volatility can weaken a nation's credibility in international negotiations, as partners become hesitant to engage in long-term agreements knowing that public sentiment could abruptly shift and reverse policy direction.

2. Populism and Reactionary Politics

Pure democracy is particularly vulnerable to populism, where leaders capitalize on public emotions and dissatisfaction to garner support. Populist leaders often promise immediate solutions to complex problems, swaying large portions of the electorate with rhetoric rather than sound, evidence-based policy. This can result in reactionary policies that lack the foresight needed to manage the intricacies of national and international trade, as well as political stability.

On the international stage, this leads to fluctuating foreign policies, where commitments to trade agreements, alliances, or global standards can be undone based on short-term political gains. Trade wars, protectionism, and the retreat from international agreements, such as climate accords, often result from populist leaders responding to popular sentiments rather than the strategic interests of the nation. While such moves might appease domestic voters in the short term, they can destabilize global trade networks, damage international relationships, and lead to retaliatory actions from other countries.

3. National Trade Policy in a Globalized World

In today's globalized economy, trade is highly interconnected and interdependent. Countries rely on complex trade agreements, supply chains, and international partnerships to fuel their economies. In a purely democratic system, where public opinion may fluctuate rapidly in response to short-term economic challenges or populist movements, trade policies are at risk of being overturned or drastically altered without sufficient analysis or understanding of the broader consequences.

For example, a country might choose to impose tariffs or pull out of a trade agreement to satisfy domestic concerns about competition or job losses in certain industries. However, these protectionist measures could backfire by increasing the cost of imports, sparking trade retaliation, and disrupting international supply chains. A popular decision to restrict foreign trade, aimed at protecting national industries, could also isolate a country economically, making it less competitive on the global stage.

This volatility is problematic for international relations as well. Other nations and international businesses prefer stability and predictability when forming partnerships, investments, or trade agreements. In a world where trade policies shift with public opinion, countries may struggle to maintain the trust and confidence needed for long-term cooperation. Businesses may hesitate to invest or expand operations in a country where trade policies and regulations can be easily influenced by political winds and electoral cycles.

4. Volatility in International Politics

In the realm of international politics, purely democratic systems can be similarly erratic. Public opinion on foreign policy is often shaped by emotions, media coverage, and immediate crises, rather than by long-term geopolitical strategies. This can lead to inconsistency in a nation's approach to diplomacy, alliances, and global governance.

For instance, international agreements on climate change, arms control, or trade can be seen as burdensome or unfair by domestic populations, leading to a popular demand to exit or renegotiate these agreements. As a result, purely democratic systems can create foreign policy whiplash, where countries engage in erratic behavior by withdrawing from or re-entering agreements based on electoral cycles rather than sustained commitment to global cooperation.

The volatility of purely democratic decisions also hinders the ability of leaders to make difficult but necessary choices that might be unpopular in the short term. Leaders who must answer directly to the electorate may avoid decisions that require sacrifice or compromise, such as adhering to environmental regulations or honoring international commitments, for fear of losing popular support. This can damage a country's reputation, disrupt alliances, and weaken its influence in global institutions.

5. The Risks of Purely Popular Approaches to Policy

Another danger in pure democracy is the over-reliance on majority opinion when it comes to complex areas such as national and international trade or foreign policy. These sectors often require expert knowledge, data-driven decision-making, and a deep understanding of global markets and geopolitics. When decisions are made purely based on what is most popular, without considering expert advice, the system becomes susceptible to uninformed decision-making. This often leads to policies that are not grounded in economic realities or strategic foresight.

For example, the rise of anti-globalization sentiments in certain democracies has led to the rejection of trade agreements and foreign investment. While these decisions may reflect immediate public concerns, such as job losses or competition from foreign markets, they often fail to address the structural changes needed in the economy or to recognize the broader benefits of international trade in terms of innovation, competition, and market access.

6. The Need for a Stabilizing Mechanism

The volatility of pure democracy in national and international trade and politics underscores the need for stabilizing mechanisms. In purely democratic systems, where policy is constantly shifting based on public sentiment, long-term planning and stability are sacrificed for short-term political gain. To prevent these issues, there is a growing argument for combining democratic governance with meritocratic elements.

A more stable system could incorporate structures that rely on experts and technocrats to advise or guide policies in areas requiring specialized knowledge, such as trade agreements, international relations, and economic strategy. By balancing democratic input with expert guidance, countries can maintain the benefits of democratic participation while ensuring that critical policies are not subjected to the volatility of public opinion or populist movements.

THE NEED FOR A SYSTEM FOUNDED ON THE INDIVIDUAL RATHER THAN GROUP MENTALITY

In traditional democratic systems, governance is often rooted in the principle of group mentality, where the majority's will guides decisions and shapes the policies that affect society as a whole. While this has provided an essential mechanism for collective decision-making, it frequently overlooks the unique needs, talents, and potential of individuals. The focus on the group can suppress individual initiative, creativity, and personal development, leading to a system that serves the collective but falls short in nurturing individual fulfillment and progress. In today's world, with growing emphasis on personal identity, autonomy, and self-actualization, there is a pressing need for a socio-political system that is founded on the individual rather than the group mentality.

1. Empowering the Individual: The Foundation of a New System

A system built around the individual recognizes that human progress, fulfillment, and well-being cannot be fully achieved by focusing solely on collective goals or majority rule. While group consensus is essential for societal functioning, an individual's talents, capabilities, and desires must also be nurtured and given space to flourish.

Such a system would be rooted in the idea that each person's development and potential are essential components of societal progress. The individual is not merely a unit in a larger collective but is, in fact, the building block upon which the system itself thrives. By emphasizing individual empowerment, this model shifts away from the group mentality that often dilutes personal freedom and autonomy. Instead, it creates a dynamic in which each individual has the opportunity to contribute to society in ways that are meaningful, fulfilling, and aligned with their own abilities.

2. Individuality as a Source of Innovation and Progress

One of the core arguments for a system founded on the individual is that individual autonomy and creativity are critical drivers of innovation and progress. When people are encouraged to pursue their passions, explore their talents, and take initiative, they contribute more meaningfully to societal advancement. In contrast, systems that prioritize group mentality often impose conformity, stifling creativity and limiting opportunities for personal growth.

Historically, the most transformative advancements in science, technology, and culture have come from individuals who were empowered to think independently. A system that emphasizes individual autonomy would create conditions where each person is free to experiment, innovate, and contribute in unique ways. It would also ensure that individuals are supported in their personal development, whether through access to education, opportunities for entrepreneurship, or mental and physical health resources.

3. The Limitations of Group Mentality

Group mentality, as seen in purely democratic systems, can often result in mob rule or majoritarian tyranny, where the needs and rights of individuals or minority groups are overlooked in favor of the majority's preferences. This system creates significant challenges, particularly when the majority's decisions are based on short-term thinking, emotion, or popular rhetoric rather than on individual well-being and long-term societal interests.

For example, a group mentality often leads to one-size-fits-all policies, which fail to account for the diversity of individuals within a society. These policies may neglect specific talents, needs, or contributions that individuals could otherwise offer. The result is a system that is rigid, prone to errors in judgment, and less adaptable to changing circumstances or innovations that arise from individual initiative.

A system founded on the individual would be designed to maximize the freedom and opportunity for each person to develop and express their capabilities. By shifting the focus to the individual, this model promotes diversity, creativity, and flexibility—qualities essential for a resilient and thriving society.

4. Redefining Responsibility: The Individual as the Center of Governance

In a system that prioritizes the individual, responsibility is shifted from the collective to the individual. This does not mean abandoning the idea of social cohesion or mutual responsibility; instead, it redefines how individuals relate to society and the state. The role of the government in such a system would be to facilitate individual development, not to dictate the paths that individuals must take.

Governance in this system would aim to create an environment where individuals are equipped to make their own decisions and pursue their own goals. This includes providing access to education, healthcare, and opportunities for personal growth while ensuring that individuals have the autonomy to shape their lives according to their own values and desires.

Rather than expecting individuals to conform to pre-set societal norms or expectations, the government becomes a facilitator of individual empowerment. Policies are designed not for the group as a whole but with the recognition that society flourishes when individuals flourish. This shift also means acknowledging that the success of society is tied to how well individuals can express their full potential, without being constrained by the pressures of group mentality or the demands of collective conformity.

5. Meritocracy as a Natural Extension of Individual-Centered Governance

A system built on the individual naturally aligns with the principles of meritocracy, where people are rewarded based on their abilities, talents, and contributions rather than their social status or adherence to group norms. In a meritocratic framework, individuals who demonstrate skill, competence, and dedication in their fields are given opportunities to lead, influence policy, or advance within the system. This prevents governance from becoming stagnant or dominated by populist trends that can erode long-term planning and development.

Democracy alone, without a meritocratic check, can devolve into a system where popularity, rather than competence, determines leadership. By integrating meritocracy, governance becomes more individual-focused, ensuring that decision-making is driven by expertise and competence rather than the whims of group mentality. This would create a system where individual excellence is both encouraged and rewarded, leading to more effective and forward-thinking leadership.

A hybrid model combining democracy with meritocracy would ensure that while individuals have the right to participate in governance through democratic representation, those with proven competence and expertise play a leading role in shaping policy in critical areas such as education, trade, healthcare, and international relations.

6. Individual Rights and Social Cohesion

A common critique of individual-centered systems is that they risk undermining social cohesion or creating excessive competition among individuals. However, this concern can be addressed by ensuring that individual rights are balanced with mutual respect and social responsibility. The idea is not to create a hyper-competitive or atomized society, but to foster a community where individual achievement and social support are interconnected.

In this model, individuals are empowered to pursue their personal goals, but with the understanding that social well-being enhances individual success. Public services, ethical guidelines, and social policies would be aimed at ensuring that everyone has the opportunity to achieve their potential, while also contributing to the broader community. Thus, social safety nets, universal access to basic services, and ethical governance would serve as the foundation for individual empowerment without sacrificing social unity.

Conclusion: The Path Forward

Shifting from a system based on group mentality to one founded on the individual represents a paradigm shift in how we approach governance, economics, and social structure. Such a system acknowledges that the true measure of a society's success lies not just in the collective outcomes but in the flourishing of each individual within it. By empowering individuals to pursue their unique talents and ambitions while maintaining social responsibility, this model provides a more flexible, adaptive, and ultimately just framework for governance.

In this approach, the individual is no longer a tool for the system but becomes the very reason for the system's existence. This recognition could lead to a more innovative, resilient, and equitable society, where personal fulfillment and social progress go hand in hand

SYSTEM OF GOVERNMENT WITH ETHICS CHAMBER

Formation and Functionality

The Ethics Chamber plays a critical role in ensuring that all governance, from local legislation to international decisions, meets high ethical standards. The formation and operation of the chamber are designed to guarantee that it remains a body of exceptional integrity, competence, and transparency. Through its peer-reviewed selection process, ongoing evaluations, and key roles in presidential selection and governance, the Ethics Chamber ensures ethical oversight, fairness, and accountability in the political system.

Initial Formation: Peer Review Process

To establish the Ethics Chamber and ensure its integrity from the start, an initial peer review process is used. This process involves identifying domain experts across various fields—such as law, economics, ethics, environmental science, and technology—and rigorously testing and reviewing their qualifications.

1. Identifying Initial Candidates:

- A panel of respected figures from different domains, unaffiliated with political interests, is selected to participate in the identification of potential members for the chamber.

- These figures, recognized for their leadership, ethical judgment, and contributions to their fields, nominate candidates who meet the criteria of expertise, ethical integrity, and public service.

2. Peer Review and Testing:

- The nominated candidates undergo domain-specific testing designed to evaluate their knowledge, decision-making capabilities, and ethical judgment.
- Existing domain leaders and experts provide feedback and conduct the review process, ensuring that the highest standards are upheld.
- Candidates are scored based on rigorous criteria, including their past achievements, ability to navigate complex ethical dilemmas, and potential for unbiased governance.

3. Voting for Initial Chamber Members:

- The panel of experts votes transparently based on the test results and assessments. The candidates who receive the majority of votes are inaugurated as the founding members of the Ethics Chamber.
- This initial peer review process ensures that the chamber starts with individuals who have a proven track record of ethical leadership and a commitment to public good.

Ongoing Selection Process: Every 6 Years

Once the Ethics Chamber is operational, the selection of future members is designed to remain fair and transparent, preserving the chamber's integrity over time. Every six years, a new selection cycle takes place, allowing domain leaders to compete for a seat in the chamber.

1. Domain-Specific Competition:

- Individuals within each domain (law, economics, ethics, etc.) who wish to serve in the Ethics Chamber participate in a structured competition.
- These candidates, selected for their expertise and leadership, undergo rigorous testing within their respective domains. The tests evaluate their knowledge, decision-making skills, ethical reasoning, and ability to navigate complex issues.

2. Transparent Testing by Existing Chamber Members:

- The current members of the Ethics Chamber play a central role in the selection process. They are responsible for overseeing the testing of new candidates, ensuring that the process is transparent and adheres to the highest standards.
- Candidates are tested on their ability to apply ethical principles in governance, handle complex scenarios, and demonstrate a deep understanding of their field.
- The scores and feedback are shared publicly, and chamber members transparently vote for the most qualified candidates based on these evaluations.

3. Selection of New Members:

- The candidates who receive the majority of votes from the existing chamber members are elected to serve a six-year term.
- This process ensures that new members are selected based on merit, competence, and their commitment to ethical governance, allowing the chamber to remain an impartial and highly effective body.

Role in Presidential Selection

The Ethics Chamber plays a pivotal role in the presidential selection process, acting as the ultimate safeguard to ensure that only the most qualified, ethical, and visionary candidates are presented to the public. This structure is designed to prevent the rise of unqualified or unethical candidates while fostering trust in the governance system.

1. House Selection of Initial Candidates

The process begins in the House of Representatives, where a diverse and representative council nominates five candidates for the presidency. These individuals are chosen based on their achievements, leadership qualities, and contributions to society. The House ensures the initial pool represents a wide range of perspectives and experiences, reflecting the nation's diversity.

2. Ethics Chamber Testing

The Ethics Chamber then subjects the five nominees to a rigorous, multi-dimensional evaluation process. This testing ensures that the final candidates not only meet technical and professional standards but also exhibit exemplary ethical character and leadership capacity. The evaluation process includes:

- **Knowledge and Expertise:** Candidates are tested on their understanding of political, social, economic, and global issues.
- They must demonstrate the ability to think critically and offer informed, innovative solutions to complex challenges.
- **Ethical Judgment:** Each candidate is assessed on their ability to navigate moral dilemmas, balance competing interests, and prioritize fairness and justice. Ethical alignment is judged not just by adherence to laws and regulations but by their demonstrated commitment to sustainability, equity, and long-term societal well-being.
- **Leadership Capacity:** Candidates undergo practical simulations to assess decision-making, crisis management, and ability to inspire and mobilize people.
- Their historical track records are thoroughly examined to ensure a consistent pattern of integrity and competence.
- **Six-Year Term Plan:** Each candidate must submit a comprehensive governance plan outlining their vision for the nation, proposed solutions for critical challenges, and key milestones for their term.

The chamber evaluates these plans for practicality, innovation, and ethical considerations, ensuring alignment with long-term national and global sustainability goals.

3. Selection of Finalists

After the Ethics Chamber completes its rigorous evaluation, the five candidates are ranked based on their performance across all criteria. The Ethics Chamber then selects the top three candidates as finalists, ensuring that only the most competent and ethically sound individuals proceed to the public elections.

- **Comprehensive Ethical and Domain-Specific Assessment:** The Ethics Chamber evaluates candidates' ethical judgment, leadership capacity, and expertise in political, social, and economic domains. This ensures that the finalists are not only ethical but also equipped to navigate the responsibilities of the presidency effectively.
- **Governance Plan Evaluation:** The Ethics Chamber thoroughly reviews each candidate's six-year term plan to assess its feasibility, ethical implications, and alignment with national and global priorities. Plans are judged for their potential to promote equity, innovation, and long-term growth while addressing critical national challenges.
- **Final Candidate Selection:** Based on these evaluations, the Ethics Chamber nominates the top three candidates as finalists for the general election. This process ensures the candidates selected are well-rounded leaders with a clear vision, moral integrity, and the technical expertise required to serve the nation effectively.
- **Transparency and Accountability:** The chamber provides a summary of its evaluations for each finalist, outlining their strengths and areas for growth. This

summary is made publicly available, ensuring that voters have a comprehensive understanding of the candidates they are choosing from.

Holistic Governance Safeguards

This structured selection process, centered on the Ethics Chamber, blends legislative oversight, ethical scrutiny, and public engagement to ensure that the nation's highest office is accessible only to those who are both capable and principled. By fostering trust, accountability, and transparency in governance, the Ethics Chamber strengthens the bond between leadership and the people it serves, paving the way for a just and prosperous republic.

ETHICS CHAMBER AS AN INTERNATIONAL CO-SIGNER FOR PRESIDENTIAL DECISIONS

A unique and critical function of the Ethics Chamber is its role as an **international co-signer** for presidential decisions, particularly in the realm of foreign policy and international agreements. This authority ensures that all major international commitments made by the president are grounded in ethical standards and maintain the nation's credibility on the global stage. Crucially, no president can unilaterally exit or renegotiate an international agreement without the co-signature of the Ethics Chamber.

1. Co-Signing International Agreements

- Before any international agreement is finalized or any treaty is ratified, the Ethics Chamber acts as an official co-signer, ensuring that the agreement aligns with ethical principles and long-term national interests.
- The chamber reviews the ethical implications of the agreement, considering the potential impact on global relations, human rights, sustainability, and fairness.
- This co-signer role prevents hasty decisions or agreements driven by political expediency, ensuring that all international commitments reflect a considered and ethical approach to foreign policy.

2. Preventing Unilateral Exits from Agreements

- One of the Ethics Chamber's key functions is to prevent the president from unilaterally exiting or renegotiating international agreements without thorough ethical consideration. If the president wishes to withdraw from a treaty or modify an agreement, the chamber must review and co-sign the decision.
- This ensures that no international commitment can be abandoned based solely on short-term political gains or populist pressures. The chamber's role as a co-signer reinforces stability and trust, both domestically and with global partners.

3. Maintaining Ethical Integrity in Foreign Policy

- By acting as a co-signer for international agreements, the Ethics Chamber plays a vital role in upholding ethical integrity in the nation's foreign policy. This co-signature requirement ensures that all decisions made on the international stage are in line with ethical principles, such as fairness, sustainability, and respect for international law.
- The chamber's involvement strengthens the consistency of foreign policy, creating long-term trust with international partners and enhancing the nation's global standing. The presence of the chamber as a co-signer signals a commitment to thoughtful, ethical decision-making in foreign affairs.

Role in Election Monitoring and Transition of Power

The Ethics Chamber also plays a crucial role in ensuring fair elections and the smooth transition of power. This oversight helps to maintain public confidence in the electoral process and the stability of governance.

1. Monitoring Elections:

- The chamber is responsible for monitoring national elections, ensuring that they are conducted transparently, fairly, and without corruption or undue influence.
- The chamber collaborates with other oversight bodies to guarantee that voting processes and campaign activities adhere to ethical standards.

2. Ensuring a Peaceful Transition:

- Once a new president is elected, the Ethics Chamber oversees the transition of power, ensuring that it occurs smoothly and without obstruction. This includes verifying that all legal and procedural requirements are met during the handover of responsibilities.
- The chamber's oversight during the transition phase helps prevent potential conflicts or power struggles, ensuring stability and continuity in governance.

Government Structure and the Role of the Ethics Chamber

The Ethics Chamber is an essential part of the larger government module, which includes the judiciary, house, senate, office of the president, and the chamber itself. Together, these branches work to maintain a balanced distribution of power and ensure that governance remains transparent, ethical, and accountable.

Ethics Chamber's Role in Government:

- The Ethics Chamber serves as an independent oversight body, distinct from other branches of government, to ensure that ethical considerations are a primary factor in all governmental actions.
    - Its power to review decisions, provide legislative guidance places it at the heart of maintaining checks and balances across the system.

Subsequent Development of Political Dynamics and Interactions

The introduction of the Ethics Chamber and a system rooted in individual empowerment creates a significant shift in the political dynamics and interactions within the proposed model, especially when compared to traditional democratic systems. These changes impact how power is distributed, how decisions are made, and how various political actors—such as elected representatives, meritocratic leaders, and the public—interact.

Here's an in-depth look at how political dynamics and interactions would evolve in the proposed system:

1. The Role of Political Leadership: Expertise and Ethics Over Popularity

In a traditional democratic system, political leadership is heavily influenced by popularity and electoral appeal. Politicians must constantly navigate public opinion, media narratives, and political campaigns to remain in power, often prioritizing short-term, voter-pleasing policies over long-term strategic goals.

In the proposed system, leadership dynamics shift dramatically with the introduction of meritocracy and the Ethics Chamber. Political leaders are no longer chosen solely based on their ability to win votes but rather on their expertise, ethical standing, and contributions to society. The Ethics Chamber acts as a guardian of these standards, ensuring that leaders are evaluated on merit and that their actions align with long-term ethical considerations rather than short-term populism.

This shift results in:

- **Less dependence on electoral cycles**: Politicians are not constantly campaigning to remain popular, allowing them to focus on governing effectively.
- **Focus on competency**: Leaders are required to demonstrate expertise in their fields (such as economics, education, or international relations), reducing the influence of charisma or emotional appeal.
- **Ethical scrutiny**: The Ethics Chamber reviews and approves major political actions, creating a new layer of accountability that ensures leaders act in the best interest of individuals and society, rather than merely following public opinion.

Political dynamics shift from a focus on appeasing the masses to one of ensuring ethical and expert-driven governance, creating a more stable political environment where leadership is based on competence, not just electability.

2. Political Interactions Between the Public and Leadership

In a purely democratic system, interactions between the public and political leaders are often reactive, driven by electoral cycles and short-term political promises. Public opinion, shaped by media, economic conditions, or social movements, often has an outsized influence on policy decisions, especially during election years. This can lead to reactionary governance, where politicians adopt policies to gain immediate favor with voters, even if those policies are not in the best long-term interest of the nation.

In the proposed system, these interactions evolve into a more deliberative process. While the public retains a voice in governance through democratic participation, their interactions with leadership are moderated by the Ethics Chamber and the meritocratic selection of leaders. This creates a more balanced relationship, where the public's input is considered alongside expert guidance and ethical oversight.

Key changes include:

- **Decreased influence of populism**: Leaders are less swayed by temporary fluctuations in public opinion because their positions are safeguarded by ethical and meritocratic standards.
- **Informed public participation**: Citizens are encouraged to engage in more thoughtful, informed dialogues about governance, as decision-making processes are more transparent and based on long-term ethical considerations rather than immediate voter preferences.
- **Citizen empowerment through personal development**: The system focuses on individual empowerment through education, opportunities for personal development, and increased access to information. This fosters a more informed and engaged electorate, reducing the need for superficial political campaigning.

The result is a more constructive interaction between the public and leadership, where both ethical standards and long-term societal interests play a more prominent role in governance.

3. Dynamics Between Political Institutions

In traditional democracies, political institutions—such as the executive, legislative, and judicial branches—often compete for power. This competition, while essential for checks and balances, can lead to gridlock or decision-making driven by partisan interests rather than a unified focus on national progress. Political parties often dominate the decision-making process, with legislation and policy heavily influenced by party agendas and electoral strategies.

In the proposed system, the Ethics Chamber adds a new dynamic, serving as an arbiter between political institutions, ensuring that their actions remain aligned with ethical principles and long-term societal goals. This fosters more cooperation between branches of government, as the Ethics Chamber serves as an objective body that evaluates decisions based on merit and ethical considerations, rather than partisan concerns.

Key changes in institutional dynamics include:

- **Reduction in partisan gridlock**: The Ethics Chamber's oversight ensures that political institutions are motivated to work together toward ethical and effective governance, reducing the influence of party politics.
- **Alignment of legislative priorities**: Policies proposed by the legislature must pass ethical review, encouraging lawmakers to collaborate on policies that are sustainable, just, and grounded in expertise. This discourages the passage of laws that are driven purely by short-term electoral gains or political posturing.
- **Judiciary guided by ethics**: The judiciary, while still independent, works in tandem with the Ethics

Chamber to ensure that rulings uphold ethical standards and protect individual rights, creating a more integrated approach to justice.

This interaction creates a more unified political system, where cooperation, ethics, and merit guide institutional behavior, as opposed to competition for political dominance or party loyalty.

4. International Relations: Ethical Diplomacy and Strategic Stability

In traditional democracies, international relations and trade policies are often shaped by public opinion and electoral cycles, leading to inconsistent or erratic foreign policies. A change in government can drastically shift diplomatic relations, trade agreements, or international commitments, creating uncertainty among global partners. Nations might enter or exit agreements based on short-term domestic pressures, undermining trust and stability in international diplomacy.

The proposed system, with the Ethics Chamber and meritocratic leadership, fundamentally changes how international interactions are conducted. In this model:

- **Ethical diplomacy** becomes a core component of foreign relations. The Ethics Chamber ensures that international treaties, trade agreements, and diplomatic efforts are aligned with ethical principles, focusing on long-term global cooperation and sustainability rather than short-term national gains.

- **Consistency in foreign policy**: Meritocratic leaders, selected for their expertise in international relations, manage diplomatic efforts based on long-term strategies rather than domestic political pressures. This results in greater stability in international partnerships, as global allies can trust that policies will not change drastically with each new election.
- **Long-term trade policies**: The focus on expertise in trade ensures that international agreements are economically sound and ethically justified, reducing the volatility that often comes with populist-driven protectionism or isolationism.

The shift in dynamics leads to more stable and predictable international relationships, built on a foundation of ethical consistency and expert-driven diplomacy, contrasting with the often reactionary foreign policies seen in traditional democracies.

5. The Ethics Chamber's Mediation of Conflicts

In traditional democratic systems, political conflict often escalates into partisan standoffs or power struggles, where winning at all costs becomes the primary goal. Disputes between political factions, institutions, or even citizens can create deep divisions, leading to a toxic political climate that undermines effective governance.

In the proposed system, the Ethics Chamber plays a crucial role in mediating political conflicts, ensuring that disputes are resolved based on ethical considerations rather than political maneuvering. The chamber's role in conflict resolution changes the dynamics of political interactions:

- **Focus on ethical resolution**: Political conflicts are evaluated and resolved by the Ethics Chamber through **objective ethical analysis**, reducing the likelihood of decisions being made for partisan advantage or populist appeal.
- **De-escalation of power struggles**: Since leadership is based on merit and ethical standing rather than political power, political actors are less motivated to engage in power struggles, fostering a more collaborative and less adversarial political environment.
- **Greater trust in the system**: With an impartial body overseeing key decisions and conflicts, the public and political actors alike develop greater trust in the system, knowing that disputes are handled with fairness and ethical rigor.

This change in dynamics reduces the level of political polarization and creates a more cooperative, solutions-oriented political environment, where conflicts are resolved with the greater good in mind, rather than partisan interests.

Shifting Political Dynamics in the Proposed System

The introduction of the Ethics Chamber and the focus on individual empowerment fundamentally reshapes the political dynamics of the proposed system. Leadership is grounded in expertise and ethics, while the public retains a meaningful role in governance through informed participation. Interactions between political institutions are more collaborative, reducing partisanship and fostering cooperation. International relations are handled with ethical diplomacy and long-term strategic thinking, ensuring stability and global trust.

Ultimately, the political dynamics shift from a popularity-driven, reactive system to one that is proactive, stable, and focused on ethical governance. The Ethics Chamber acts as a safeguard against the volatility and unpredictability often seen in purely democratic systems, ensuring that individual empowerment and societal progress remain central to governance.

Conclusion

In an era marked by rapid societal and global changes, the need for a governance model that is both ethically grounded and meritocratic has never been more pressing. The Ethics Chamber Independent Government Circuit offers a compelling vision for how modern governance can evolve to meet the complexities of the 21st century. By placing the individual at the heart of the system while ensuring that leadership is selected based on merit and ethical standards, this model balances democratic participation with expert oversight.

The Ethics Chamber's structure fosters long-term stability, ethical consistency, and public trust. Its rigorous selection process ensures that only the most capable and ethical individuals serve in leadership roles. The blend of transparency, public engagement, and merit-based leadership ensures that governance remains responsive to the people while adhering to high ethical standards.

This system represents a bold step toward addressing the volatility of pure democracy and the limitations of group-centric governance. By combining the strengths of democracy and meritocracy, it lays the foundation for a society where individuals are empowered, leadership is accountable, and decisions are made for the long-term benefit of the nation and the global community.

As we move forward, the Ethics Chamber offers a framework for creating not only a fairer and more ethical government but one that is capable of navigating the complex challenges of our time. This model demonstrates that it is possible to maintain the balance between individual fulfillment, collective good, and global responsibility—ultimately paving the way for a governance system that is just, transparent, and sustainable for future generations.

SOCIAL FRAMEWORK

Free Access to Basic Necessities

A cornerstone of the proposed socio-economic model is the guarantee of universal access to essential services, ensuring that every citizen, regardless of background or economic status, can enjoy a baseline of security and well-being. This system is designed to eliminate the disparities that arise from unequal access to fundamental resources such as healthcare, food, and housing.

Universal Healthcare

The system provides universal healthcare, offering both physical and mental health services to all citizens. By ensuring that healthcare is available and free for everyone, the system addresses one of the key drivers of inequality—disparities in health outcomes. Access to healthcare is no longer dependent on income, employment, or geographic location, but is treated as a basic human right. This reduces preventable diseases, improves mental health outcomes, and enhances the overall well-being of the population.

Food Security

In this model, the state ensures food security for all citizens. A robust, state-supported network guarantees access to nutritious and sufficient food, thereby eliminating hunger and malnutrition. Access to quality food is not only fundamental for physical health but also provides a solid foundation for mental well-being. This system eradicates food deserts, supports sustainable agricultural practices, and ensures that no one in society is left without the resources to maintain a healthy diet.

Affordable Housing

Affordable housing is another critical element of this system. The government provides safe and secure housing for all citizens, ensuring that no one is left without shelter. This guarantee of affordable housing serves to stabilize living conditions for the population, drastically reducing homelessness and housing insecurity. By removing the economic pressure of unaffordable rent or housing costs, individuals are free to focus on personal development and community engagement, rather than mere survival.

Benefits of Free Access to Basic Necessities

1. **Enhanced Quality of Life:** By ensuring access to universal healthcare, food security, and affordable housing, this system dramatically enhances the quality of life for all citizens. Individuals no longer need to worry about the basic necessities of survival, allowing them to pursue personal, professional, and communal growth. Families experience reduced financial strain, and the general stress associated with meeting these essential needs is alleviated.

2. **Reduced Inequality:** Access to basic necessities helps create a more level playing field. Social and economic disparities—often exacerbated by unequal access to healthcare, food, and housing—are significantly diminished. Everyone, regardless of their background or socioeconomic status, has access to the fundamental resources needed for a dignified life, reducing systemic inequalities and fostering greater social cohesion.

SOCIAL ORGANIZATION: A PSYCHOLOGICAL APPROACH TO INDIVIDUAL DEVELOPMENT FROM BIRTH

To create the best system for human development, the approach must involve a concept of "structural multi-directional facilitation," where external influences and structures are designed to provide as much support and opportunity as possible from various angles. This means creating environments that nurture potential, provide diverse pathways for growth, and expose individuals to a broad range of experiences and information. By being actively involved in shaping these external conditions, the system increases the probabilities of positive outcomes, giving people the tools, access, and framework they need to explore and develop in multiple directions.

However, at the same time, it is crucial to interfere as little as possible on a developmental level, allowing individuals the freedom to grow subconsciously without imposed constraints. This "non-interference" in the personal development process ensures that human growth occurs organically and naturally, without forcing specific outcomes or over-structuring paths of development. By minimizing direct interference in developmental processes, individuals can achieve optimal subconscious development, discovering their own trajectories and unique potentials without being confined by external pressures. This delicate balance between facilitation and non-interference creates a dynamic system that supports human flourishing without stifling it.

The goal of an overall structure, whether psychological or social, should not be to rigidly transform chaos into order, but rather to create a system where order and chaos can coexist harmoniously. Chaos, in this sense, represents the unpredictability, innovation, and potential for growth that arises from uncertainty, while order represents stability, structure, and coherence. By allowing both to exist side by side, individuals and societies can maintain flexibility and adaptability while also providing enough stability to sustain progress. Instead of eliminating chaos, systems should embrace it as a source of potential, ensuring that neither extreme—absolute order nor absolute chaos—dominates entirely.

The goal of the social structure also is to create a system where malleable, decentralized hierarchies can naturally form while preventing long-term social oppression and disparity. In such a structure, hierarchies would not be rigid or oppressive but flexible and adaptable, allowing individuals to rise or shift within them based on merit, contribution, or circumstances. This fluidity in hierarchy ensures that no fixed power structures dominate indefinitely, fostering inclusivity and reducing the likelihood of entrenched inequality or social stagnation.

By decentralizing power and allowing these hierarchies to form dynamically, the system would aim to distribute opportunities and resources more evenly, preventing the concentration of wealth, privilege, or authority in the hands of a few. It encourages a balance between leadership and equity, promoting collaboration and ensuring that as society evolves, no single group remains in a position to oppress others or create lasting disparities. This approach supports continuous social mobility and evolution, aligning with a vision of fairness and dynamic development.

Additionally the goal also includes enabling both trait-specific groups and cross-trait groups to form and interact on a grand developmental level. This approach fosters diversity in personal and group development by allowing individuals with similar traits to cultivate their unique strengths, while also promoting interaction across different trait groups to encourage collaboration, innovation, and shared growth.

By facilitating both intra-group and inter-group dynamics, this structure supports a richer, more interconnected social ecosystem where people can grow within their natural tendencies while benefiting from the exchange of ideas and skills with those of different strengths. This model aims to cultivate a balance between specialization and collaboration, fostering both individual growth and collective advancement without stifling any one trait group.

The social organization in this system is deeply rooted in human psychology, recognizing the need for a structured environment that supports the development of the individual from birth. Rather than relying on traditional family structures, which often vary in terms of resources and capabilities, this model places each individual under state security from birth. This guarantees that every child, regardless of their background, is given the tools and support needed for their optimal development.

State Security from Birth: Ensuring Equal Opportunities

From the moment a child is born, they are placed under the care of the state, ensuring that all children have equal access to healthcare, education, and social resources. The system is designed to prevent the inequities that often arise from family-based social structures where wealth, education, and social standing can determine a child's future. Instead, this model provides a level playing field, ensuring that all children grow up in an environment that supports their physical, emotional, and intellectual development.

This state security ensures that no child is disadvantaged by their family's socioeconomic status. With the state acting as the primary custodian, children are protected from the fluctuations of individual family circumstances, such as financial instability, neglect, or lack of access to quality education. The state's primary role is to provide a nurturing and stable environment, allowing children to focus on their growth, exploration, and self-discovery without the constraints that traditionally come from unequal familial resources.

Structured Developmental Pathways

The developmental journey from childhood to adulthood is designed with clear, structured pathways that cater to the psychological and social needs of the individual. As children grow, they are introduced to a series of developmental milestones aimed at fostering both personal autonomy and a sense of social responsibility. The state provides tailored education, mentorship, and emotional support to ensure that each individual reaches their full potential.

1. **Early Childhood Development:** During the early stages of life, children are provided with nurturing care that focuses on emotional security, cognitive development, and socialization. Early childhood education is centered around critical thinking, creativity, and ethical values, ensuring that children build a solid foundation for later stages of learning. This period is crucial for instilling confidence, curiosity, and the ability to form healthy social bonds.

2. **Adolescence and Exploration:** As children enter adolescence, the system shifts to encourage more self-directed exploration of interests and potential career paths. At this stage, individuals are provided with personalized educational opportunities that align with their emerging talents and passions. This phase also

introduces them to real-world problem-solving, community engagement, and leadership development, allowing them to practice the skills needed for societal participation.

3. **Adulthood and Integration into Society:** Upon reaching adulthood, individuals transition into their respective societal groups, based on their abilities, contributions, and interests. This process is guided by a series of assessments and mentorship programs that help individuals find their ideal societal role—whether in public service, creative industries, sciences, or entrepreneurship. The integration process is gradual and supportive, ensuring that every adult enters society as a well-rounded, capable, and ethically grounded contributor.

Guided Transition into Societal Roles

One of the key features of this system is the guided transition from childhood to adulthood. The state plays an active role in helping individuals identify their strengths, interests, and passions while providing the resources necessary for them to develop these attributes fully. The process is not rushed but rather unfolds in stages, ensuring that every individual has ample time and support to make informed decisions about their future societal role.

- **Strength-Based Integration:** Rather than forcing individuals into predetermined roles, the system encourages strength-based integration into society. This means that individuals are placed in roles that best suit their unique capabilities and passions, promoting personal fulfillment and societal efficiency.

- **Ethical and Psychological Foundations:** Throughout this developmental journey, the state emphasizes ethical education and emotional well-being, ensuring that individuals not only have the technical skills required for their roles but also the emotional intelligence and moral grounding necessary for ethical decision-making.

Benefits of the State-Oriented Development Model

This state-centric approach to social organization offers several advantages over traditional family-based systems:

1. **Eliminating Disparity at Birth:** By removing the variability in resources, education, and care that comes with family-based upbringing, this system ensures that no child is disadvantaged by their birth circumstances. Every individual, regardless of background, is provided with the same opportunities for growth and success.

2. **Reducing Parental Pressure and Social Stress:** Parents are relieved of the overwhelming responsibilities associated with raising children in unequal or stressful circumstances. This allows parents to focus on their own personal development, career advancement, and emotional well-being, creating healthier family dynamics overall.

3. **Optimal Psychological Development:** The state provides a stable, nurturing environment that is scientifically designed to support optimal psychological

development. By focusing on the emotional, intellectual, and social needs of the individual, the system ensures that all citizens are prepared to contribute meaningfully to society.

4. **Strong Social Cohesion:** By guiding individuals into societal roles based on their strengths and interests, the system fosters social cohesion and a sense of belonging. Individuals are integrated into the fabric of society through a process that aligns personal development with the needs of the community, creating a stronger, more unified social structure.

Conclusion: A Psychological and Ethical Foundation for Society

The proposed social organization represents a radical shift in how societies support and nurture their citizens. By placing individuals under state security from birth and providing them with structured developmental pathways, this model ensures that every person is given the tools they need to succeed—both personally and socially. The emphasis on human psychology, ethical grounding, and strength-based societal integration offers a vision of a society where individuals are empowered to thrive in their unique capacities, while also contributing meaningfully to the collective good.

This approach eliminates many of the disparities and insecurities that arise from family-based systems, replacing them with a state-supported framework designed to foster individual growth, well-being, and social harmony from birth to adulthood.

FAMILY AS COMPANIONS: A COLLABORATIVE APPROACH TO PARENTHOOD

In this social model, the traditional understanding of family is redefined to foster a more collaborative and supportive approach between parents and the state. Couples who wish to start a family are not simply given full authority over the upbringing of their children. Instead, they are recognized as companions and co-guardians, sharing the responsibility for their child's development with the state. This structure ensures that each child receives consistent, high-quality care and education in line with societal values and ethical standards.

Companions and Co-Guardians: A New Form of Parenthood

The status of companions represents a partnership between parents themselves and between parents and the state. Couples who achieve family status, after undergoing rigorous parental training programs, are recognized as having a shared role in raising their children, with responsibilities that go beyond traditional parental roles. The designation of parents as companions symbolizes mutual respect, cooperation, and shared commitment to the child's well-being.

- **Companionship in Parenthood:** The relationship between the two parents is framed as one of equal partnership, with both taking on the role of nurturing the child in a way that aligns with the state's ethical standards. In this model, parenting is viewed as a shared journey, in which both individuals contribute equally to the child's emotional and intellectual growth.

- **Co-Guardianship with the State:** As co-guardians, parents do not have sole authority over the decisions related to their child's upbringing. Instead, they share this authority with the state. This ensures that all children are raised in a manner that is consistent with the broader goals of society—namely, fostering individuals who are ethical, well-educated, and socially responsible. The state's involvement provides a safeguard, ensuring that children are not subject to the variabilities that can arise from unequal access to resources, education, or parenting skills.

Parental Acknowledgment of State Authority

Upon achieving family status, parents must formally acknowledge the state's authority over the well-being and development of their children. This acknowledgment is a key element of the social contract between the family unit and the state. It ensures that while parents are entrusted with raising their children, they must do so within the parameters set by the state to guarantee the child's optimal development.

- **State's Role in Child Development:** The state provides a framework for child development that emphasizes ethical behavior, intellectual growth, and emotional resilience. It ensures that all children, regardless of their background, are given the resources and support necessary to thrive. This state oversight includes access to education, healthcare, mental health services, and other key developmental resources that might otherwise be unequally distributed in traditional family structures.

- **Parental Role in Child Nurturing:** Parents play a vital role in emotional nurturing and day-to-day care, but they do so within a system that ensures every child receives the same baseline of support. Parents are expected to provide love, care, and guidance while adhering to state guidelines that prioritize the child's development. This dual role—where parents nurture while the state provides structural support—ensures that children are raised in a stable and ethically sound environment.

Training and Preparation: Becoming a Family

One of the unique aspects of this model is the requirement that couples wishing to start a family must undergo a comprehensive training program. This program is designed to prepare them for the challenges of parenthood, focusing on practical parenting skills, ethical education, child development, and the state's role in the child's upbringing.

- **Comprehensive Parental Training:** The training program is rigorous and covers a wide range of topics, including child psychology, educational techniques, and ethical decision-making. This ensures that parents are well-prepared to raise their children in a way that aligns with the state's ethical standards. The training also teaches parents how to collaborate with the state in the co-guardianship of their children, fostering a sense of partnership rather than control.

- **State Supervision During Child Development:**
  Throughout a child's development, the state remains
  involved, providing oversight and ensuring that the
  child's education and upbringing align with societal
  goals. Parents are supported by the state but also held
  accountable to the standards set during their parental
  training. This system helps avoid the risks of children
  being raised in environments that might not fully
  support their intellectual or emotional needs due to
  economic or social constraints.

Aligning Child Development with Ethical and Educational Standards

The main purpose of this shared guardianship model is to
ensure that every child's development aligns with ethical,
educational, and developmental standards set by the state. By
placing the child's well-being as the central concern, the model
creates a consistent and equitable upbringing for all children,
reducing the risk of disparity caused by unequal family
environments.

- **Ethical Education:** The state's ethical standards ensure
  that children are raised with a strong sense of moral
  responsibility, respect for others, and social
  accountability. Parents, as companions, are tasked with
  nurturing these values in the home, but within a
  framework that ensures all children receive consistent
  ethical guidance.
- **Equitable Educational Opportunities:** Parents must
  ensure that their child's education aligns with state

standards, guaranteeing equal access to high-quality education. This avoids the uneven educational opportunities that often arise from socioeconomic differences in family structures. Children, regardless of their family's wealth or background, are provided with the same level of educational support, preparing them to contribute meaningfully to society.

A Supportive Partnership Between Families and the State

This model's strength lies in its ability to create a supportive partnership between families and the state. Parents are not burdened with the entire responsibility of raising a child in isolation, but are instead supported by the state in ensuring that their child has access to the best possible resources for their development. This partnership promotes a more holistic approach to child-rearing, where parents focus on emotional nurturing and day-to-day care, while the state ensures access to education, healthcare, and social development.

- **Parental Support:** The state provides ongoing support to parents, offering resources such as mental health services, educational counseling, and financial assistance when needed. This ensures that parents are not overwhelmed by the challenges of raising children, allowing them to focus on nurturing their child's emotional well-being.
- **State Oversight:** The state ensures that all children receive consistent and equal care, monitoring their progress and stepping in if necessary to address any deficiencies in their upbringing. This creates a safety

net for children, preventing them from falling through the cracks due to family struggles or challenges.

Benefits of the Family as Companions Model

1. **Equal Opportunities for All Children:** This system ensures that all children, regardless of their family's socioeconomic status, receive the same level of care, education, and ethical guidance. By making the state a co-guardian, the model removes the disparities often caused by unequal family circumstances.
2. **Reduced Parental Stress:** Parents are relieved of the overwhelming responsibility of raising a child entirely on their own. With the state acting as a partner in child-rearing, parents can focus on providing emotional support without the fear of being unable to meet their child's educational or developmental needs.
3. **Consistent Ethical Standards:** The state's oversight guarantees that all children are raised with the same ethical standards, creating a more just and equitable society. Parents, as companions, are tasked with instilling these values in the home, ensuring that their children grow up as responsible and ethical members of society.
4. **Supportive Parental Training:** The comprehensive training provided to couples ensures that parents are well-prepared for their roles as caregivers. This creates a generation of parents who are knowledgeable, equipped, and ready to guide their children within a structured, supportive framework.

Conclusion: A New Paradigm of Family and Society

The family as companions model represents a fundamental shift in how society views the role of parents and the state in child-rearing. By fostering a partnership between parents and the state, this system ensures that children are raised in an environment that prioritizes their development, well-being, and ethical education. This collaborative approach not only reduces the burdens on parents but also creates a more equitable and consistent upbringing for all children, ensuring that every individual has the opportunity to succeed.

THE EFFECTS OF REMOVING THE ROOTS OF INJUSTICE ON SOCIETY

One of the central goals of this proposed socio-economic system is to eliminate the roots of injustice—whether they stem from economic disparity, social inequality, or systemic biases. By doing so, this model not only addresses long-standing societal challenges but also profoundly reshapes how individuals experience life. The effects of removing these roots of injustice are transformative and reach deep into the core of individual and societal existence.

1. Effects on Individualization

In a society free from the roots of injustice, the emphasis shifts from group-based dynamics of survival and competition to the flourishing of the individual. With equitable access to resources, education, and opportunity, individuals are no longer defined by their background or social class. The result is a new form of individualization,

where people are free to express their true selves without the limitations imposed by systemic inequalities.

- **Empowered Self-Expression:** Individuals can pursue personal passions, interests, and goals without fear of discrimination or limited access to opportunities. This freedom to self-actualize creates a diverse, vibrant society where individuals thrive based on their unique contributions.
- **Diminished Pressure to Conform:** The removal of injustice allows for a reduction in the societal pressure to conform to rigid norms or expectations. Individuals can choose their own paths, unconstrained by the need to fit into predefined roles dictated by socioeconomic status, race, or other external factors.

2. Effects on Mental Illness and Depression

Mental health is often tied to external stressors, many of which are rooted in social inequality and injustice. By removing these root causes, this model offers a profound reduction in mental illness, particularly depression and anxiety.

- **Reduced Social Stressors:** Injustices such as poverty, discrimination, and unequal access to healthcare often exacerbate mental health issues. By eliminating these stressors, the system creates an environment where individuals can experience emotional stability and well-being.
- **Enhanced Mental Health Support:** Universal access to mental health services ensures that individuals

struggling with psychological challenges are supported. With resources available to everyone, mental health becomes a priority, leading to a significant reduction in depression, anxiety, and stress-related disorders.

- **Increased Sense of Belonging:** A society that is inclusive, just, and free from systemic oppression fosters a stronger sense of belonging among its members. Individuals feel valued and respected, which helps prevent the isolation and alienation that often contribute to mental health issues.

3. Effects on Abortion Rates

In a system where the state takes responsibility for child-rearing and provides unconditional support for both parents and children, the decision to terminate a pregnancy is significantly impacted. With reduced financial and emotional burdens, more individuals may feel equipped to carry pregnancies to term.

- **Increased Willingness to Have Children:** With the state providing the bulk of child-rearing responsibilities, potential parents face fewer obstacles when it comes to having children. The pressures of financial instability, lack of access to healthcare, and societal challenges are mitigated, making it easier for individuals to consider having children.
- **Lower Abortion Rates:** The presence of a strong social safety net reduces the circumstances under which abortion is often sought, such as financial insecurity or an inability to provide for a child. As a result, abortion

rates are expected to decline, particularly among those who would otherwise feel unprepared to raise a child without the system's support.

4. Effects on Individual Life Experience

By eliminating injustice and providing unconditional access to resources, the individual's experience of life is fundamentally altered. Life satisfaction increases, as individuals no longer face the constant struggle for survival and security.

- **Enhanced Life Satisfaction:** When individuals are no longer burdened by basic survival needs, they have the freedom to explore personal fulfillment, creativity, and relationships. This leads to a deeper sense of satisfaction in life, as people are free to pursue what truly matters to them.
- **Freedom from External Limitations:** The removal of systemic barriers allows individuals to experience life without the constraints of societal injustice. This leads to greater opportunities for self-actualization and the pursuit of personal passions, resulting in a more fulfilling and enriched life experience.

5. Effects of a Lifelong Unconditional Safety Net with Unlimited Resources

A society that provides an unconditional safety net—ensuring access to healthcare, education, housing, food, and support—creates a profound sense of security for its citizens. The knowledge that one's basic needs will always be met allows individuals to live free from fear and uncertainty.

- **Increased Risk-Taking and Innovation:** Knowing that their fundamental needs are guaranteed, individuals are more likely to take creative risks, innovate, and pursue entrepreneurial ventures. Without the fear of failure leading to poverty or instability, society becomes more dynamic and forward-thinking.
- **Greater Emotional and Psychological Security:** The unconditional safety net provides emotional and psychological stability. Individuals do not have to live with the stress of potential job loss, health crises, or financial collapse. This leads to lower levels of anxiety and a society where people feel supported and secure throughout their lives.

6. Removing Stress from Parents: Increased Life Satisfaction

One of the most significant impacts of this system is the removal of the stress traditionally associated with parenting. By taking on the bulk of child-rearing responsibilities, the state alleviates many of the pressures that parents face, allowing them to focus on personal growth and fulfillment.

- **Reduced Parental Stress:** Parents are no longer overwhelmed by the financial, emotional, and logistical challenges of raising children. The state's involvement in child-rearing allows parents to enjoy the experience of nurturing their children without the associated burdens of work-life balance, financial insecurity, or educational challenges.
- **Increased Parental Fulfillment:** With reduced stress, parents can focus on personal fulfillment, career development, and self-care. This leads to a higher sense of life satisfaction, as parents are not solely defined by the demands of parenthood but are supported in their journey by a broader societal structure.

7. Removing Drivers of Criminality: Enhanced Social Stability

One of the most significant impacts of this system is the elimination of disparities that fuel criminal behavior. By building a healthier psychological foundation and redefining success beyond material profit, the state fosters a society where individuals can thrive without resorting to crime.

- **Elimination of Disparities:** The system removes economic and social inequalities by providing universal access to resources such as education, healthcare, and housing. This ensures that all individuals have an equal opportunity to succeed, reducing the desperation and resentment that often lead to criminal behavior.
- **Healthy Psychological Foundation:** By addressing the root causes of stress, trauma, and marginalization, the

system promotes mental and emotional well-being. This creates a stable environment for individuals to develop positive relationships, self-worth, and a sense of belonging, reducing the psychological drivers of crime.

Conclusion: The Comprehensive Impact of Removing Injustice

The removal of injustice at its roots—whether through economic, social, or systemic reforms—ushers in a transformative era for both individuals and society. By ensuring that every citizen has access to unlimited resources and unconditional support, the system fosters a society that is emotionally, psychologically, and socially stable.

Mental illness and depression are reduced, abortion rates decline as potential parents feel secure in their ability to care for a child, and life satisfaction increases across the board. Individuals experience life with greater freedom, opportunity, and fulfillment, knowing that their basic needs are met and that they are supported in their personal development.

The unconditional safety net not only removes the stress from parents but also allows society to flourish as people are free to pursue passions, take risks, and innovate without fear of failure. This model creates a future where individuals are truly empowered, and society thrives on the collective strength of its citizens living in harmony, free from the limitations imposed by injustice.

GOVERNMENTAL COMMUNAL ESTABLISHMENTS: TAILORING COMMUNITIES FOR SPECIFIC NEEDS AND PREFERENCES

A critical aspect of the proposed social model is the creation of governmental communal establishments, designed to cater to the unique needs and preferences of various groups within society. These communities are structured to provide optimal environments for individuals at different stages of life, with specific goals, interests, or identity preferences. By tailoring communal living around family life, elderly care, entrepreneurial pursuits, college environments, and individual identity, the system fosters personal fulfillment, social support, and overall well-being.

1. Family-Oriented Communities

Family-oriented communal establishments are designed to support households with children, focusing on providing a stable, nurturing environment where families can thrive. These communities are equipped with resources that alleviate common pressures associated with child-rearing and family life, such as state-sponsored childcare services, educational support, and access to parental training programs.

- **Supportive Infrastructure:** These establishments offer access to schools, healthcare facilities, recreational spaces, and family counseling services, ensuring that families have the resources they need to raise healthy, well-rounded children. Parents are also provided with guidance and training to help them navigate the complexities of modern parenting, ensuring they feel supported in their roles as co-guardians within the system.

- **Community Cohesion:** Family-oriented communities foster a sense of cohesion and mutual support by connecting families with shared values and goals. This not only strengthens individual families but also creates a network of collective care, where parents and children can benefit from a strong, stable community foundation.

2. Elderly-Oriented Communities

With an aging population, elderly-oriented communities are designed to offer a dignified, engaging, and supportive environment for seniors. These establishments focus on ensuring quality of life for the elderly by providing access to healthcare, social services, and mental health support, while encouraging active participation in community life.

- **Healthcare and Support Services:** Residents have access to specialized healthcare tailored to their needs, including in-home care, medical facilities, and wellness programs. Additionally, these communities offer opportunities for continued learning, social interaction, and cultural engagement, helping seniors maintain a sense of purpose and belonging.
- **Intergenerational Connections:** These communities also encourage intergenerational connections, allowing seniors to mentor younger members of society and share their life experiences. Such interactions foster social cohesion and provide the elderly with

opportunities to remain actively engaged in the broader community.

3. Entrepreneurial-Oriented Communities

Entrepreneurial-oriented communities are designed to nurture creativity, innovation, and business development. These hubs focus on fostering economic growth by providing resources for startups, small businesses, and entrepreneurial ventures. By creating environments where collaboration, mentorship, and innovation thrive, these communities serve as incubators for the next generation of leaders and innovators.

- **Business Resources and Networking:** Entrepreneurs in these communities have access to shared workspaces, financial resources, and mentorship programs from established business leaders. These establishments also offer legal, financial, and technical support to help startups succeed, driving innovation and economic prosperity.
- **Collaboration and Innovation:** The culture of collaboration within these communities encourages entrepreneurs to share ideas, collaborate on projects, and build networks that foster innovation. This environment creates a vibrant ecosystem where businesses can grow and thrive, contributing to the broader economy.

4. College-Oriented Communities

Designed to cater to the needs of students and academics, college-oriented communities focus on fostering intellectual growth, social engagement, and professional development. These establishments provide students with access to educational resources, mental health support, and a structured environment that encourages academic success and personal growth.

- **Academic and Career Development:** Students in these communities benefit from access to state-of-the-art educational facilities, including libraries, research centers, and mentorship programs that prepare them for careers in their chosen fields. These communities also focus on creating work-study opportunities and internships, ensuring that students have practical experience in their areas of study.
- **Cultural and Social Engagement:** Beyond academic life, college-oriented communities encourage cultural enrichment and social activities, helping students develop well-rounded personalities. These communities offer a mix of academic rigor and social engagement, ensuring that students are prepared to thrive in both their professional and personal lives.

5. Identity-Oriented Communities

In recognition of the diverse identities and preferences within society, identity-oriented communities are built around individuals' personal, cultural, and social identities. These communities offer spaces for self-expression and foster acceptance, where individuals can explore their identities in an environment that supports their unique experiences and perspectives.

- **Tailored Support Systems:** These communities offer access to services and support that reflect the specific needs of their members. Whether based on cultural heritage, sexual orientation, or personal interests, identity-oriented communities create spaces where individuals feel valued, respected, and understood.
- **Diversity and Inclusivity:** By promoting diversity and inclusivity, these communities foster a sense of belonging and personal empowerment. Members are encouraged to engage in civic activities, celebrate their identity, and contribute to the larger societal framework.

The Role of Communal Establishments in Society

By building governmental communal establishments around specific life stages, preferences, and interests, the system supports individuals in a more personalized and effective manner. This tailored approach not only improves individual well-being but also strengthens society by ensuring that each person has access to resources, community, and opportunities that match their unique needs.

These establishments are critical in fostering social cohesion, promoting personal development, and creating a more inclusive and adaptable society. Each community, while tailored to specific groups, contributes to the overall societal goal of individual fulfillment and collective progress, ensuring that no one is left behind in the pursuit of a better, more harmonious world.

Economic Benefits of Predesignated Communities

The creation of predesignated communities—such as family-oriented, elderly-oriented, entrepreneurial-oriented, college-oriented, and identity-oriented communities—offers not only social and personal advantages but also significant economic benefits. These specialized communal establishments create economic efficiencies, promote sustainable growth, and foster innovation by concentrating resources, support, and opportunities in a way that maximizes each group's potential. Below are the key economic advantages of this model:

1. Increased Productivity Through Specialization

Predesignated communities allow for the specialization of resources, services, and infrastructure, which in turn boosts overall productivity. By focusing on the specific needs of each community, resources are deployed more efficiently, and individuals are provided with targeted support that enhances their productivity and contributions to the economy.

- **Tailored Resources and Services:** For example, entrepreneurial communities are equipped with the resources necessary to foster innovation and business development, such as shared workspaces, business mentorship programs, and access to venture capital. This concentration of resources leads to faster innovation cycles and greater economic output, as entrepreneurs can focus on growth rather than navigating complex, generalized systems.
- **Workforce Readiness: College-oriented** communities, on the other hand, produce a highly skilled and

prepared workforce by providing students with the education, mentorship, and practical experience they need to enter the job market. This helps bridge the gap between academic training and real-world employment, ensuring that students are better equipped to contribute to the economy immediately after graduation.

2. Cost-Effective Public Services

By grouping individuals with similar needs and life stages, predesignated communities allow governments to deliver public services more efficiently. Instead of spreading resources thinly across a broad, diverse population, services can be concentrated where they are most needed, reducing the cost of service delivery while improving outcomes.

- **Efficient Healthcare and Social Services:** In elderly-oriented communities, the concentration of elderly individuals allows for specialized healthcare and support services that are both cost-effective and better tailored to their specific needs. The government can allocate resources more efficiently, reducing the cost of long-term care and improving health outcomes, thus reducing the burden on the overall healthcare system.
- **Focused Infrastructure Development:** By concentrating populations with similar needs, governments can also optimize infrastructure development. For example, in family-oriented communities, investments in education, parks, and childcare facilities serve a concentrated population,

maximizing the return on infrastructure spending while addressing the specific needs of families.

3. Promotion of Innovation and Economic Growth

Entrepreneurial-oriented communities play a key role in promoting innovation and economic growth. By creating hubs where entrepreneurs, business leaders, and innovators can collaborate and share resources, these communities serve as incubators for new ideas, businesses, and industries.

- **Business Ecosystems:** The proximity of startups, investors, and resources within entrepreneurial communities leads to the creation of vibrant business ecosystems that attract further investment and talent. As startups succeed, they contribute to job creation, industry diversification, and economic growth, benefiting both the local economy and the national GDP.
- **Job Creation and Market Expansion:** The success of businesses within these communities contributes to broader market expansion and increased demand for goods and services. The innovations developed in these hubs can also lead to the creation of entirely new industries, driving long-term economic growth and competitiveness in the global market.

4. Attraction of Foreign and Domestic Investment

Predesignated communities, particularly entrepreneurial-oriented and college-oriented ones, have the potential to attract foreign and domestic investment by establishing themselves as centers of excellence. When resources, talent, and infrastructure are concentrated in these specialized hubs, investors are more likely to see these communities as high-potential areas for investment.

- **Attracting Venture Capital:** Entrepreneurial hubs can become magnets for venture capital, as investors look to back innovative startups with strong growth potential. This influx of investment capital not only benefits individual businesses but also strengthens the broader economy by creating jobs and fostering new industries.
- **Global Talent Magnet:** College-oriented communities can attract international students and academic talent, generating significant economic benefits. International students often contribute to the local economy through tuition fees, living expenses, and long-term employment, making these communities valuable contributors to both local and national economic growth.

5. Long-Term Economic Sustainability

Identity-oriented and family-oriented communities contribute to long-term economic sustainability by creating environments where people can thrive both personally and professionally. By aligning community resources with the specific needs of individuals, these communities encourage long-term residency and economic stability, reducing the costs associated with population turnover and transient populations.

- **Reduced Social and Economic Disparities:** These communities create inclusive environments where individuals feel supported and valued, leading to reduced social and economic disparities. As residents feel a stronger connection to their communities, they are more likely to remain engaged in the local economy, contributing to long-term economic resilience.
- **Increased Quality of Life and Economic Participation:** As individuals in family-oriented or identity-oriented communities experience a higher quality of life, they are more likely to engage productively in the economy, whether through employment, entrepreneurship, or civic participation. This leads to a more engaged, economically active population, further driving growth and development.

6. Sustainable Infrastructure and Resource Management

Predesignated communities provide an opportunity for governments to develop sustainable infrastructure that meets the specific needs of each community while reducing the overall environmental impact. By concentrating infrastructure investments, governments can implement green technologies, energy-efficient buildings, and public transportation systems that reduce waste and lower the cost of managing public utilities.

- **Green Infrastructure in Entrepreneurial and Family-Oriented Communities:** For instance, entrepreneurial communities might be developed with a focus on sustainable, green infrastructure that minimizes environmental impact, while family-oriented communities can benefit from investments in clean energy and green spaces that enhance the quality of life.
- **Efficient Use of Resources:** The efficient use of resources in these communities ensures that government investments in infrastructure yield higher returns over the long term. With reduced waste and lower operational costs, governments can achieve both economic and environmental sustainability.

A Model for Economic Efficiency and Growth

The creation of predesignated communities tailored to specific societal groups offers significant economic advantages. By concentrating resources, services, and infrastructure around the needs of different populations, governments can achieve greater efficiencies in public service delivery, promote innovation and economic growth, attract investment, and create long-term economic sustainability. These communities not only enhance individual well-being but also contribute to a more robust, resilient, and thriving economy.

Conclusion

The proposed social framework presents a revolutionary approach to organizing society, one that places the individual at the center of a carefully structured system designed to provide unconditional support from birth. By ensuring universal access to basic necessities such as healthcare, education, food, and housing, the system eliminates the roots of economic and social injustice, fostering a society where inequality is minimized and opportunity is available to all.

This model is built on the foundation of human psychology, recognizing the importance of nurturing individual development from childhood to adulthood within a secure and supportive environment. The state's role in child-rearing, along with comprehensive parental training programs, ensures that every child has the best possible start in life, free from the disparities traditionally associated with family-based upbringing. As individuals progress through life, they are guided and supported by the state in their personal development, contributing to a more cohesive, stable, and ethically grounded society.

By removing the stress of survival and offering an unconditional safety net, the system not only improves the overall quality of life but also reduces mental illness, depression, and social isolation. Parents are relieved of the overwhelming pressures of raising children on their own, allowing them to focus on personal fulfillment and career advancement, leading to greater life satisfaction.

The result is a society where individual life experiences are enriched, where abortion rates decline due to increased security, and where individuals are free to pursue their passions and contribute meaningfully to the collective good. This model lays the foundation for a future where justice, equality, and opportunity are not aspirations but realities, and where every citizen is empowered to lead a life of fulfillment, creativity, and purpose.

In essence, this social framework reimagines the relationship between the individual and the state, building a society that not only addresses the systemic issues of the past but also creates a harmonious, ethical, and inclusive future for all.

A STABLE CURRENCY FOR A NEW WORLD

Introduction to the Development of Mediums of Exchange

Since the dawn of human civilization, the necessity for trade and the exchange of goods has been fundamental to societal growth. Early human communities relied on barter systems, where goods and services were directly exchanged based on perceived equal value. However, this system quickly revealed its limitations, primarily due to its inefficiency. Barter required a double coincidence of wants—both parties had to possess exactly what the other wanted at the same time. This inefficiency gave rise to the need for a medium of exchange that could facilitate trade in a more flexible and scalable manner.

The Emergence of Commodities as Early Mediums

As societies advanced, the first step toward more efficient trade was the use of commodity money—items that held intrinsic value in themselves, such as livestock, grain, or precious metals.

Gold and silver, in particular, became widely accepted across various cultures due to their durability, divisibility, and inherent scarcity. These commodities served as symbols of value, simplifying the exchange process by providing a universally accepted medium that could be traded for goods and services.

Despite its efficiency, the use of commodity money carried significant challenges, including storage, transportation, and the inability to precisely match the value of goods. As economies and trade networks expanded, the need for more portable and convenient mediums of exchange became increasingly apparent.

The Invention of Coinage and Early Currency

Around the 7th century BCE, the invention of coinage revolutionized the concept of money. Civilizations such as the Lydians and Greeks began minting coins from metals like gold, silver, and bronze, with standard weights and government-imposed values. These coins not only represented the value of the underlying metal but also served as an early form of state-backed currency. The introduction of coinage marked a significant step toward more standardized and regulated economic systems.

Coinage, with its precise denominations and widespread acceptance, facilitated more efficient trade across regions and empires. It also allowed governments to centralize economic control and manage taxation, leading to the early development of monetary policies.

The Shift to Paper Money and Credit Systems

As trade networks grew and economies became more complex, the limitations of metal-based currency became apparent. Transporting large quantities of coins was cumbersome, and the supply of precious metals was often insufficient to meet the needs of expanding economies. This led to the development of paper money, which originated in China during the Tang and Song dynasties (7th-13th centuries CE) and spread globally over the centuries.

Paper currency represented a significant shift in the understanding of money. No longer tied to the intrinsic value of the metal itself, money now operated on a system of trust and government authority. Governments and financial institutions issued paper notes backed by reserves of gold or other valuable commodities. This made trade easier and more scalable, as large transactions could be conducted without the need to physically transfer valuable metals.

Alongside the development of paper money, credit systems began to emerge. Merchants and traders, particularly in the early modern period, developed systems of promissory notes, bills of exchange, and other forms of credit. These instruments allowed for the deferred payment of goods and services, further increasing the fluidity and efficiency of trade.

The Rise of Fiat Currency and Modern Economic Systems

The next major development came with the widespread adoption of fiat currency—money that holds value because a government declares it to be legal tender, rather than because it is backed by a physical commodity like gold. The abandonment of the gold standard in the 20th century, particularly after the collapse of the Bretton Woods system in 1971, marked a new era where currencies were primarily based on government authority and economic performance.

Fiat currency allowed governments to have more flexibility in managing their economies. Through monetary policies, such as adjusting interest rates or controlling the money supply, governments could influence inflation, employment, and overall economic growth. This system, however, is inherently dependent on trust—trust in the government's ability to manage the economy, trust in the value of money, and trust in the future stability of the nation.

The Digital Age and Cryptocurrency

In recent years, the emergence of digital currencies and cryptocurrency has begun to reshape the conversation around mediums of exchange. Cryptocurrencies like Bitcoin, built on blockchain technology, offer decentralized, secure, and digital forms of currency that operate outside of traditional banking systems. While still in its early stages, cryptocurrency represents a potential shift toward a new form of medium of exchange—one that relies on digital verification rather than state backing.

These innovations point to an evolving understanding of value and exchange, where trust in institutions may eventually be replaced by trust in technology and decentralized systems. However, cryptocurrencies face challenges of scalability, volatility, and regulation, making their long-term viability as global mediums of exchange uncertain.

Conclusion: Toward a New Global Standard

The history of the mediums of exchange reflects a constant evolution—one driven by the need for efficiency, scalability, and trust. From bartering and commodity money to coinage, paper money, and fiat currency, each step has represented a shift in how societies understand and assign value to goods and services. As we move into the digital age, new forms of currency and economic models are emerging, forcing us to reconsider what money truly represents.

MONEY AS THE CONTINUITY OF LIFE

In our world, money functions as more than a mere medium of exchange or a resource to satisfy needs—it's the lifeblood that sustains and shapes human continuity on individual, generational, and societal levels. Money, in essence, is the tangible representation of continuity in life itself, anchoring our present to our future and connecting individual existence to the collective human experience.

Survival and Security

At its core, money represents survival and the assurance of tomorrow. The ability to earn, save, and spend imparts a sense of security, grounding our existence and providing the foundation for planning, building, and sustaining life. For individuals, financial stability mitigates the anxiety of uncertainty, offering a buffer against the unpredictable and giving rise to a profound sense of stability. Without it, the future becomes a source of distress, and the most basic needs of survival are under threat. In this way, money not only satisfies immediate needs but also serves as the mechanism through which the continuity of existence is secured and envisioned.

The Bridge Between Generations

Money is a connector of generations, a thread that weaves individual lives into the fabric of a larger story. Through the transfer of wealth, knowledge, and opportunity, it becomes a vehicle for passing down contributions, achievements, and aspirations from one generation to the next. A parent's sacrifice, the investments made, and the opportunities funded become legacies that extend beyond a single lifetime, supporting the continuity of family, culture, and society. As each generation builds on the previous one, money becomes a medium for transferring not only material wealth but also the values and potentials necessary for the future.

The Life-Force of Economic Systems

In the broader economic and social landscape, money functions as the life-force that drives resources, powers innovation, and catalyzes societal development. Every aspect of modern life—productivity, health, education, art, and infrastructure—depends on the flow of capital. In this sense, money is a circulating energy, an undercurrent that sustains the dynamic systems allowing societies to evolve and prosper. As a life-force, it channels collective energy, guiding it toward shared goals and growth, making development and progress tangible and achievable.

Psychological and Social Anchors

Money also plays a central role in shaping identity, social belonging, and personal meaning. For individuals, it is tied to self-worth, ambition, and life purpose, affecting everything from self-image to relationships. Financial stability often brings a sense of control and influence, shaping one's place within society and guiding aspirations and interactions. On a societal level, money structures the interactions between individuals and groups, creating frameworks of power, hierarchy, and responsibility. It is more than currency—it is a symbol of trust, a metric of value, and a shared belief in our capacity to thrive collectively.

Conclusion: Money as Life Continuity

By understanding money as the continuity of life, we see it as more than just a means to an end. It is a system through which we sustain existence, shape identity, and cultivate legacy. Money not only enables the survival of individuals but also advances the collective journey of humanity. It is both the energy that fuels societies and the scaffolding that supports our most enduring aspirations, serving as the bridge between the present moment and the future possibilities we strive to create. This continuity is what makes money an irreplaceable force, a form of life force that encapsulates the essence of both human fragility and potential.

In recognizing money as the continuity of life, we redefine its role—not merely as an economic tool, but as the means through which we manifest existence, connection, and progress across time.

TRUST DEFINED AS CONTINUITY

Trust is the invisible thread that binds societies, systems, and individuals together. In its essence, trust is far more than belief or confidence—it is reliance on continuity. It is the foundation upon which relationships, economies, and governance systems are built, ensuring stability and predictability in an otherwise uncertain world.

At its core, trust is the bridge between the present and the future. It embodies the belief that what exists today—be it a system, an institution, or a relationship—will persist, remain functional, and uphold its promises. This reliance on continuity allows individuals to plan, act, and collaborate with the assurance that their efforts will not be rendered meaningless by systemic or relational failure.

In economic terms, trust is the cornerstone of value. Currency, for instance, is not just a medium of exchange but a representation of collective trust in the future. A stable currency reflects the confidence of individuals and institutions in the continuity of governance, production, and trade. When trust erodes—whether through corruption, instability, or systemic inequity—the continuity of economic systems is disrupted, often leading to chaos and collapse.

Governance too finds its legitimacy in trust. Effective governance is not merely the enforcement of laws or the administration of policies; it is the cultivation of trust through transparent, equitable, and sustainable practices. Systems that prioritize continuity—by protecting individual dignity, ensuring equitable access to resources, and fostering long-term stability—naturally generate trust. Conversely, when governments fail to ensure continuity, trust breaks down, giving rise to unrest and disintegration.

On a personal level, trust is the anchor of the human psyche. It provides the stability needed to navigate relationships, pursue goals, and maintain a cohesive sense of self. When trust is broken—whether through betrayal, systemic failure, or trauma —it disrupts this continuity, severing the connection between the individual and their sense of security.

Conclusion

Trust, when understood as continuity, becomes a universal principle that transcends domains and scales—from personal relationships to global governance. It is not an abstract ideal but a living force that sustains life, systems, and societies. By embedding continuity into the very fabric of human systems, we create structures that are not only stable but regenerative, ensuring that trust is preserved across generations.

CURRENCY AS LIFE CONTINUUM

Redefining Currency

The concept of currency as life continuum transforms money from being a mere tool of exchange or a measure of value into a force that sustains and dignifies human existence. In this framework, currency is no longer a neutral metric but an embodiment of the flow of energy, resources, and trust that ensures life's continuity. By aligning economic systems with humanity's most fundamental need—to live, thrive, and realize potential—currency becomes a direct reflection of life itself.

This redefinition transcends conventional economic models, offering a vision where fairness, justice, and sustainability are not abstract ideals but systemic realities.

Fairness and Justice

At its core, this redefinition places universal access to life continuum at the heart of fairness and justice. Currency, seen as a medium for sustaining life, brings forth ethical principles that naturally emerge to govern its use. In this context, justice is not about retrospective redistribution but ensuring that no individual is excluded from accessing the resources and opportunities necessary for survival and growth. Fairness ceases to be an afterthought and becomes a proactive design principle, one that eliminates exploitation, inequality, and systemic failures by its very structure.

Equity Through Need and Potential

Equity within this model emerges as an outcome of access to the life continuum, achieved by balancing the potential and needs of individuals. This approach transcends simplistic equality, focusing instead on tailoring access to resources to maximize both individual and collective flourishing. Those with greater needs receive more support, while individuals with untapped potential are empowered to contribute meaningfully to society. This dynamic balance between need and potential ensures that equity is not just about uniformity but about fostering fair opportunity and sustainable growth for all.

Trust as the Foundation

This framework transforms trust into the foundation of economic and social systems. Currency becomes a direct reflection of collective confidence in the future—a tangible measure of how societies value life and are willing to invest in its continuity. Trust, in this model, is not static but a dynamic interplay between individuals, systems, and the environments they inhabit. It ensures that resources are allocated sustainably and equitably, eliminating excess and waste while creating a regenerative flow of resources that mirrors the natural cycles of life.

A Unified Framework

Currency as life continuum creates a unified ethical and economic framework where governance, economics, and morality are deeply interconnected. Ethical governance facilitates access to the life continuum for all, ensuring that systems operate with fairness and equity at their core. Economics, in turn, becomes a mechanism for balancing individual needs with collective sustainability. Within this framework, equity, fairness, and justice are no longer peripheral considerations but essential components of the system's design, preserving every individual's dignity and enabling their potential to be fully realized.

The Ethical Domain as Foundation

In this vision, the ethical domain is not an abstract overlay on economic systems; it is a direct extension of life's inherent dignity. Fairness, justice, and equity are measured by how effectively systems enable access to the life continuum while fostering a balance between individual needs and collective potential. Economic structures are transformed into custodians of human dignity, ensuring that no one is left behind and that future generations inherit a world of sustainability and opportunity.

Conclusion: A New Civilization

Ultimately, the concept of currency as life continuum reimagines the very foundation of human systems. It offers a model for a more just, equitable, and sustainable civilization, one that integrates fairness, trust, and sustainability into every decision. By doing so, it transforms not only how societies allocate resources but also how they understand and value life itself.

VALUE AS REALIZED POTENTIAL

Value, at its core, is the actualization of potential. It is not an inherent or static attribute but an emergent quality that arises when latent possibilities are brought into meaningful existence. This perspective redefines value as dynamic and transformative, deeply tied to the processes of growth, expression, and fulfillment across all dimensions—economic, human, and systemic.

In economic terms, value reflects the utility or benefit derived when resources, services, or systems fulfill their potential. A tool's worth is realized when it solves a problem; a service's value emerges when it meets a need. Currency itself, often perceived as an abstract medium of exchange, becomes a representation of trust in the future potential that individuals, systems, and societies can actualize. Value, therefore, is not fixed but flows as potential is realized, making it an active force that drives economies forward.

From a human perspective, value is deeply tied to the realization of individual and collective potential. A person's talents, creativity, and capacities hold immense latent value, but this value is only realized when opportunities and resources allow for their expression. Equity, in this framework, becomes essential—ensuring that every individual has fair access to the means of unlocking their potential, contributing to a society where collective value flourishes.

Ethically, the realization of potential reflects the dignity and worth of existence. A just society is one that enables value to emerge by removing barriers to potential. In this sense, fairness and sustainability are mechanisms to ensure that latent possibilities are not wasted due to systemic inefficiencies or inequities. Justice itself becomes an act of cultivating value by empowering individuals and systems to transform potential into tangible outcomes.

Value as realized potential also ties intimately to the dimension of time. Potential exists as a promise of the future; value is created in the present when that promise is fulfilled. This mirrors the flow of life itself—a continuous process where latent possibilities manifest, creating meaning and progress. By aligning economic, ethical, and governance systems with this principle, we move closer to structures that honor human dignity, sustain equity, and foster collective growth.

Conclusion

In reimagining value as realized potential, we redefine the very fabric of human systems. Value becomes a living, dynamic process—a bridge between what could be and what is. This perspective compels us to design economies and societies that focus not on static accumulation but on the continuous realization of potential. Such a shift lays the foundation for systems that are just, equitable, and regenerative, ensuring that every individual and community can contribute to and benefit from the flourishing of humanity. Ultimately, this redefinition of value isn't just a new way of thinking—it's a path of action to create a world where potential becomes reality, and life itself becomes the ultimate measure of worth.

MONEY AND SUBCONSCIOUS TRUST IN FUTURE

Money can be seen as a tangible manifestation of trust in the future. At its core, money represents a system of deferred value, where people believe that the currency they hold today will hold value and purchasing power in the future. This belief is not just about the currency itself but about the future of society, the stability of institutions, and the collective agreement that money will continue to be a reliable medium of exchange. Without this underlying trust, money loses its value, and economies can spiral into crises of confidence, as seen in instances of hyperinflation or financial collapse. In this sense, money is more than just a tool of exchange—it's a symbol of collective faith in the continuity of value and societal stability.

This trust in the future, however, operates on a much deeper, subconscious level. From an individual perspective, trust in the future functions as a psychological mechanism that drives behaviors, decision-making, and overall life planning. When people trust that tomorrow will be better or at least as stable as today, they are more likely to invest, save, and make long-term commitments. This subconscious belief in a favorable or stable future is what propels individuals to engage with the present in meaningful ways, seeking to build and protect their personal wealth. When this trust is eroded, individuals become more risk-averse, often pulling back from investment and spending, which can stagnate both personal and broader economic growth. Consequently, the circulation of money in an economy directly reflects individual trust in the future—when confidence is high, money flows more freely, spurring growth; when confidence wanes, money circulation slows, leading to economic stagnation or contraction.

On a systemic level, this subconscious mechanism of trust reverberates through financial institutions, markets, and government policies. The value of money is deeply intertwined with the trust people place in the systems that regulate it. For example, central banks play a crucial role in maintaining this trust by ensuring monetary stability, managing inflation, and acting as lenders of last resort. When these systems are perceived as reliable, they reinforce the collective belief in the future. If confidence in these institutions falters, whether due to political instability, corruption, or economic mismanagement, the entire financial system can become unstable, reflecting how systemic trust and money are intertwined. Additionally, the overall health of an economy, including its growth rate, employment levels, and innovation, mirrors the systemic trust in the future, with robust economies demonstrating confidence and weak ones reflecting doubt.

At a societal level, trust in the future shapes collective behavior and societal structures. Economies that foster trust in future opportunities tend to innovate and grow, as individuals feel secure enough to take risks, start businesses, and contribute to societal progress. This societal trust is built on cultural, political, and economic foundations that allow for the fluid exchange of ideas, goods, and money. Societies with a strong sense of collective trust in the future are more resilient and better equipped to adapt to change, whereas societies that lose this trust often face stagnation, social unrest, or collapse. Moreover, when systemic and individual trust in the future is reflected in a healthy economy, money circulates efficiently, supporting the development of these societies. In contrast, in economies where trust is weak, people are less inclined to spend or invest, which causes a slowdown in circulation and a subsequent economic decline.

The subconscious nature of trust in the future is reflected in how societies prioritize development and growth. From infrastructure projects to education systems, societal investment in the future is a direct result of this underlying trust. Without a belief in a stable or prosperous future, governments and societies would struggle to justify large-scale, long-term investments. This future-oriented mindset is essential for human advancement and is mirrored in how money is used as both a measure and an enabler of value across time. As money flows through the economy, its circulation serves as a barometer of collective trust, indicating the degree to which people believe in future growth and stability.

Ultimately, money functions as both a practical tool and a psychological indicator of societal and systemic health. The deeper, subconscious mechanism of trusting in the future is fundamental to how individuals, institutions, and societies interact with money. When this trust is secure, economies thrive, and societies flourish; when it falters, the very fabric of financial and social systems can unravel. Money and trust in the future are inextricably linked, each reinforcing and shaping the other across multiple levels of human existence, with the circulation of money and the overall economy serving as reflections of systemic and individual trust in the future.

Thus comes the need for a currency that not only reflects but also sustains the true representation of money as trust in the future. Such a currency would go beyond mere economic functionality and become a direct embodiment of collective belief in societal progress, stability, and the continuity of value. It would be tied to factors that genuinely reflect human development, ecological sustainability, and technological advancement, creating a deeper alignment between monetary systems and the real forces that drive the future forward. In this way, the currency itself would become a stabilizing force, reinforcing trust not just in financial systems, but in the future as a whole, ensuring that as we move forward, the underlying trust that propels societies and economies remains robust and resilient.

The relationship between money and trust in the future operates on multiple levels—individual, systemic, and societal —shaping and reflecting the health of economies and human progress. Money is not just a medium of exchange but a symbol of our collective faith in the continuity of value and the stability of the future. On a subconscious level, this trust drives personal behaviors and broader economic flows, influencing how individuals invest, save, and spend. Systemically, trust in institutions like central banks and financial markets determines how effectively economies function and how money circulates within them. Societally, this trust shapes long-term investments and the potential for innovation and growth. The circulation of money in an economy becomes a mirror of this underlying confidence, with robust flows indicating a healthy future outlook and stagnation revealing cracks in this collective trust. Ultimately, money serves as both a practical and symbolic expression of trust in the future, interweaving with the subconscious mechanisms that drive human actions and societal stability. When trust is strong, economies and societies prosper; when it falters, the consequences ripple through all layers of existence.

THE DOLLAR'S THRONE AND THE NEED FOR A NEW BENCHMARK – THE CASE FOR MVC

Since the dismantling of the gold standard and the establishment of the Bretton Woods system, the US dollar has transcended its role as a national currency to become the primary global metric of value. Nearly every asset, from oil to gold, is benchmarked against it, making the dollar an invisible anchor for the world economy. This dominant position has enabled the United States to act as the gatekeeper between the physical economy and the abstract realm of value. The dollar has evolved from being simply a currency into a conceptual standard, defining worth across global trade, investments, and economic health.

However, as global economies grow increasingly complex and interdependent, this reliance on a single national currency reveals its vulnerabilities. The question now emerges: Can we envision a system where value is not measured by the dollar alone but by a new, universally representative metric? The Medium Value Currency (MVC) is a concept born from this necessity, designed as a neutral and resilient benchmark unshackled from the policies and interests of any single nation, grounded in universal metrics of value that reflect global productivity and sustainability.

The Unit of Measurement Defines the Entire Dimension

When we choose a unit of measurement, we're not just picking a reference point—we're defining how that entire dimension operates and is understood. The unit creates the boundaries, rules, and meaning for the dimension. In other words, the unit doesn't just quantify things within that dimension; it creates the framework that allows the dimension to exist as a coherent system of meaning.

For example:

- In physical measurement, meters give rise to the dimension of length, defining how distance and space are understood.
- In economic terms, a currency as a unit of measurement gives rise to the dimension of economic value, determining how goods, services, and wealth are perceived and quantified.

The Bretton Woods Shift: Redefining the Dimension of Value

Under the pre-Bretton Woods system, gold was the unit of measurement for value, meaning the entire dimension of value was defined by gold. This setup established a stable, universally recognized reference point, where currency was a representation of the fixed value of gold:

- **Gold as the Defining Unit**: With gold as the unit, value was concrete and stable. The entire economic dimension was grounded in something physically scarce and universally accepted, so value was perceived as inherent and tangible.
- **Fixed Meaning of Value**: Since gold measured currency, value was directly tied to something objective and limited, making the concept of value stable and constrained by tangible resources.

However, Bretton Woods flipped the scales by establishing currency, specifically the U.S. dollar, as the unit of measurement for value. This fundamentally changed the entire dimension of economic value:

- **Currency as the New Unit, Defining a New Dimension**: When currency (the dollar) became the measuring unit, value itself was no longer grounded in a physical asset but in the abstract trust in fiat currency. This shift redefined value as something dynamic, influenced by policies, interest rates, and economic conditions, not by tangible resources.

- **A Dimension Based on Fiat Trust**: The dollar, as the unit of measurement, created a new economic dimension where value was defined by the stability and strength of U.S. monetary policy. This change allowed for flexibility and growth but also introduced risk, as value now depended on fluctuating factors rather than fixed assets.

The Shift in Unit Redefined Economic Reality

With this understanding, we can see the full impact of the Bretton Woods flip:

1. **Unit Sets the Dimension's Nature**: By moving from gold to the dollar as the unit, the nature of the economic dimension transformed from fixed and asset-backed to flexible and policy-driven. This redefined what value meant, making it an abstraction governed by trust rather than physical resources.

2. **Dependency on Currency as the Foundation of Value**: The new dimension, with currency as the defining unit, created an environment where all value calculations and economic interactions were tied to the dollar's stability. This dependency meant that global value hinged on fiat trust in the dollar, and thus, the stability of this entire dimension of value was now vulnerable to the health of the U.S. economy.

3. **Loss of Objectivity in Value Measurement**: By flipping the unit to currency, value became subjective, open to inflation, and reliant on national policies. The dimension of value, once objective and universal with

gold, became fluid and variable with the dollar, shaping a world where value could expand or contract with policy decisions and market sentiment.

The Dollar's Evolution from Currency to Concept

The dollar's influence is a product of deliberate strategy and historical momentum. With the Bretton Woods agreement establishing it as the world's reserve currency and the petrodollar system embedding it in global energy markets, the dollar has become more than a national asset. Its transition from a weighed value system (where physical assets, like gold, measured wealth) to a numerical value system (where value exists as numbers on a balance sheet) allowed the dollar to redefine value on a global scale. In this system, the US dollar became the arbiter of worth, fundamentally shaping the global economy's dimension of value.

However, this dependence on the dollar poses risks. By linking the value of all global assets to the health of the US economy, nations worldwide become vulnerable to US monetary policy and economic shifts. A single nation's currency should not define the value reality for the world, especially as we face an era of ecological and economic challenges that demand a truly global, stable standard. The Medium Value Currency (MVC) is introduced as a new benchmark designed to reflect collective human potential and progress without dependency on any one national economy.

Balanced System of Economic Energy

Printing money without producing more goods or services is like redistributing energy within a closed system—it doesn't create new economic energy but spreads the existing "value energy" more thinly across a larger supply. In physics, energy cannot be created or destroyed, and similarly, increasing the money supply doesn't increase real wealth. Instead, it dilutes the economic power of each currency unit, much like spreading a fixed amount of energy over a wider area reduces its intensity. This shift benefits some (like debtors who repay loans with devalued money) but diminishes the purchasing power for others, especially those holding cash or fixed incomes.

The energy theory applied to economics suggests that currency, much like energy in a closed system, cannot simply be created without adding real value or productivity. Currency only holds stable value when it reflects the economy's actual output—goods, services, and technological advancements. When new money is printed without a corresponding increase in productive activity, it dilutes the "economic energy" represented by currency, leading to inflation as more money chases the same amount of goods. Thus, true economic growth depends on productive work and innovation, which generate the real value that currency should represent, preserving the stability of its purchasing power.

Workers play a crucial role in this energy cycle, as they are the primary creators of value. Through their labor, skills, and innovations, workers generate wealth in the form of goods and services, effectively creating the "energy" that fuels economic growth. The income workers receive from their labor enables them to participate in the economy as consumers, driving demand for goods and services. This demand encourages further production, creating a balanced flow of economic energy. The cycle is self-sustaining as long as productive activity aligns with the currency supply, ensuring that the money circulating in the economy represents real, tangible value produced by the labor force.

In a balanced system, currency grows only in proportion to productive output, preventing the excess currency supply that would otherwise lead to inflation. This equilibrium between supply (production) and demand (worker-driven purchasing power) creates a stable economic environment. By aligning currency growth with productivity, the economy upholds the Law of Conservation of Economic Value, where currency represents genuine economic energy rather than speculative or artificially inflated value. This balance ensures sustainable growth, as each unit of currency maintains its worth, preserving purchasing power and supporting a stable, resilient economy.

While GDP measures the total value of goods and services produced within an economy, a currency's value also depends on the demand generated within that economy. GDP alone reflects the supply side—how much is being produced—but the true stability and worth of a currency require a healthy demand side as well, primarily driven by the purchasing power and consumption needs of the workforce and population.

A productive economy does more than just increase GDP; it also empowers workers and consumers to spend, creating a natural, sustainable demand for goods and services. This demand maintains a balanced economic flow, where the currency circulates in alignment with real economic activity. The more people participate in the economy—spending on products, investing in services, and saving for the future—the more the currency's value is grounded in actual economic interactions, rather than in speculative or external factors.

Therefore, currency valuation depends on both GDP and the internal demand generated by the economy's productivity. When these two forces—supply (GDP) and demand (internal purchasing power)—are aligned, the currency becomes more resilient, maintaining its value without excessive inflation. This dual foundation of GDP and domestic demand creates a stable economic environment, where the currency accurately reflects the productive and consumption dynamics of its host economy.

Why MVC? A New Standard of Value Defined by MVI Metrics

The MVC seeks to redefine value within a unique framework where 1 MVC represents the full sum of all MVI metrics—a complete index of global productivity, ecological health, technological progress, and human development. This means that 1 MVC embodies the entire dimension of value within the global economy. By setting this fixed point, MVC establishes a finite, balanced system of value, creating proportional relationships between all economic activities and their impact on global metrics. Each component of the MVI metrics contributes to this total of 1 MVC, forming a dynamic yet bounded system that reflects the real and relative value generated across economies.

To create the stability needed for MVC, this value would be pegged to universally recognized assets like gold and oil. Gold provides MVC with a stable, preserved value, representing wealth that endures over time. Oil, on the other hand, embodies dynamic economic output, connecting MVC to the energy and productivity that drive modern economies. By combining the stored value of gold with the active value of oil, MVC creates a balanced anchor grounded in real assets and reflective of human progress. This dual-peg system strengthens MVC as a global standard by making it responsive to both historic trust and current productivity.

Transitioning from the Dollar to MVC: A Parallel Pathway

Replacing the US dollar as the world's primary benchmark will require gradual integration of MVC through a parallel existence alongside the dollar. Rather than an immediate switch, MVC would be introduced as a supplementary standard, allowing economies to transition slowly and adjust to this new metric of value. Over time, as MVC gains credibility and liquidity, it can increasingly take on roles traditionally dominated by the dollar, creating a smooth, non-disruptive shift.

During this period, MVC would function in tandem with the dollar, with both currencies existing within the global financial system to provide a dual framework of value. Nations, businesses, and financial institutions could opt to conduct transactions, trade, and investments in either currency, giving them a choice that gradually shifts market trust and liquidity toward MVC. As MVC's usage becomes widespread, dollar liquidity would effectively flow into the MVC system, creating a transfer of value that steadily establishes MVC as the primary global standard.

This parallel existence would ease the global transition by ensuring stability, mitigating risks associated with currency upheaval, and allowing time for the MVC system's infrastructure and trust to solidify. Eventually, the liquidity currently tied to the dollar would be absorbed into MVC, enabling it to fully replace the dollar as the primary global benchmark, marking a new era in value definition and economic resilience.

Envisioning a Sustainable Global Economy with MVC

In an MVC-based global economy, value is not defined by any single nation's economic policy but by a collective index of human productivity, ecological health, and development. By setting 1 MVC as the total of all MVI metrics, the system encapsulates all dimensions of human progress in one universal benchmark, where every transaction, investment, or economic activity aligns with this dimension of value. Balancing currency generation and burning to maintain coherence within the full score of MVI metrics ensures that value remains tied to real, measurable progress across diverse sectors.

This system not only balances stored and active value through its dual anchor to gold and oil, but it also aligns with sustainable growth. As productivity increases, MVC can respond, allowing value to grow proportionally within its defined metrics. By focusing on metrics tied to real economic health and ecological sustainability, MVC offers an alternative to the cyclical boom-and-bust patterns that have characterized dollar-based finance. Instead, the global economy would be rooted in long-term resilience, where value reflects collective progress rather than speculative gains.

Conclusion: MVC as a Path to a Balanced and Sustainable Future

For decades, the dollar has been the backbone of global finance, but its role as the ultimate measure of value is not without consequence. As we face growing global challenges, the need for a neutral, sustainable, and universally representative benchmark becomes clear. The MVC offers a pathway to reimagine value as a measure of collective human achievement, grounded in universally recognized assets like gold and oil and structured within a finite, balanced dimension where 1 MVC equates to the full score of MVI metrics.

This framework marks a profound shift toward a future where value is defined by shared goals and progress, rather than the economy of a single nation. Adopting MVC as the global benchmark allows us to move toward an economy that values sustainability, balance, and equity, where growth is aligned with the true needs of humanity. Through a careful parallel transition with the dollar, MVC could become the cornerstone of a resilient global economy, ultimately absorbing the liquidity and trust once held by the dollar. In doing so, MVC redefines the concept of value to reflect both our present and potential as a global society, setting the stage for a prosperous, sustainable future that aligns with humanity's highest aspirations.

THE COLLAPSE OF THE CURRENT ECONOMIC MODEL: A PATH TO UNIMAGINABLE CONSEQUENCES

The global economy today is a complex web of interdependent systems that have evolved over centuries. These systems, built on the foundations of fiat currency, supply and demand, and various geopolitical factors, are what sustain the modern world. However, if the current economic model were to collapse, the consequences would be catastrophic. Civilization, as we know it, would face an unprecedented shock to resource availability, plunging much of the world into harsh poverty and famine.

In such a scenario, reverting to older mediums of exchange, such as gold, would not provide a viable solution. Gold, which once served as the foundation of monetary systems due to its scarcity, is no longer capable of representing the vast scale of the modern global economy. The sheer amount of value present in today's global marketplace far exceeds what gold could feasibly back. Furthermore, the reality is that most of the world's gold is concentrated in the hands of a few powerful institutions and nations, making it inaccessible to the broader population. Even if a return to gold-backed currency were possible, there simply wouldn't be enough to represent the true value of global trade and commerce.

The collapse of the current system would be more than just a financial crisis—it would be the collapse of centuries of accumulated value. The modern economy is not just a system of present value but a construct built on borrowing from the future. Investments, future growth, and the expectation of continuous development are what sustain this economic framework. If this structure crumbles, all of the projected future value would vanish, leaving nothing to comparatively represent value in any tangible form. The result would be a descent into economic chaos, where the mechanisms that underpin global trade, finance, and even basic resource distribution would disappear.

The Impracticality of Returning to Gold

Gold's historical role as a medium of exchange stemmed from its natural scarcity, which made it a reliable store of value. However, this was during a period when the world economy was much smaller and less interconnected. Today, the complexities of global trade, technological innovation, and the sheer volume of economic activity demand a more nuanced and scalable system of value representation. A return to gold would ignore the holistic understanding of value and exchange that modern economies have developed.

The historical circumstances that led to the creation of modern monetary systems, particularly the adoption of floating currencies like the U.S. dollar, were shaped by very specific economic and geopolitical conditions. The world was transitioning from commodity-backed currencies to fiat money, which allowed for greater flexibility in managing national economies. These circumstances are not replicable, and any attempt to revert to previous models would be doomed to failure. The understanding of "mediums of exchange" has evolved, and the prerequisites that made gold-based systems functional in the past no longer exist.

The Fragility of the Global Economic System

The current global economic system is held together by confidence in currency—the belief that money holds value because society has collectively agreed that it does. While this system works under normal conditions, it is inherently fragile. Should confidence in this system falter, the consequences would ripple across every aspect of human life. Resource shortages, inflationary spirals, and the collapse of international trade would lead to a breakdown in the very systems that keep society functioning.

Without a functioning medium of exchange, even basic necessities like food, water, and medicine would become scarce, and the infrastructure that ensures their distribution would disintegrate. In the absence of a stable currency, there would be no reliable way to measure or exchange value, leading to a breakdown in trust and cooperation. Governments would struggle to provide for their citizens, and global poverty would skyrocket. Civilization would teeter on the edge of collapse, unable to sustain the complexity of modern life without a stable and agreed-upon system of value.

Conclusion: The Need for a New Model

The collapse of the current economic system would not only erase the value of money as we know it but also the very mechanisms that sustain modern civilization. A return to older systems of value, such as gold, is neither feasible nor reflective of the current complexities of the global marketplace. The holistic understanding of value and exchange that we have developed requires a new approach—one that can adapt to the demands of the modern world and ensure stability in the face of economic challenges. As we explore the potential for a new global currency system, such as the Medium Value Currency (MVC), it becomes clear that the future of money must reflect the realities of today's interconnected world.

THE LOGIC BEHIND THE SYSTEM

In the current global economy, growth is largely driven by resource extraction and consumption, fueling a cycle where prosperity hinges on finite resources and ecosystems that are rapidly diminishing. This model, rooted in short-term gain, often disregards the long-term effects on ecological stability and the continuity of life itself. The outcome is an economic structure that feeds on life and resources to sustain itself, depleting the very foundations on which it depends. The logic of this system has led us to the brink of ecological and societal collapse, where progress is too often synonymous with depletion.

The system envisioned here is rooted in an entirely different logic, one that sees value as the product of life continuity and resource expansion. It is an economic framework designed not to consume, but to create, regenerate, and balance. By reframing the purpose of economic activity, this system aims to establish a self-sustaining loop, where every action taken within the economy contributes to a net-positive effect on the world. Rather than operating as a machine that extracts value from the environment, this model transforms the economy into an organism that fosters life, using the concept of value to support renewal and resilience.

Shifting from Extraction to Regeneration

At the heart of this system is a fundamental shift in perspective: value is no longer tied solely to accumulation or immediate utility but is instead linked to sustainability and renewal. Here, value emerges from the system's ability to contribute to the continuity of life and the replenishment of resources. This means that every economic activity is measured not just by what it produces, but by how it sustains the environment and fosters collective growth. In practical terms, this translates to a model where economic rewards are aligned with activities that regenerate resources, improve ecosystems, and support the well-being of future generations.

The guiding logic of the system is based on proportionality and balance. Rather than seeking limitless expansion, it promotes growth that's aligned with the earth's capacity to sustain. This approach prevents overconsumption and sets a baseline for sustainable expansion. Growth, in this context, is a process of enhancing life's capacity—of creating more with less by increasing efficiency, durability, and resilience in every sector. The emphasis shifts to quality over quantity, encouraging innovations that make the most of resources rather than depleting them.

The Role of Life Continuity and Resource Expansion

The emphasis on life continuity and resource expansion places humanity's collective future at the forefront of economic value. By designing a system where value is derived from expanding resources, whether through technological innovation or ecological conservation, the economy becomes a vehicle for progress that benefits both people and the planet. This is a long-term view of prosperity, where each generation contributes to a legacy of abundance, not scarcity.

Within this system, innovation is encouraged in sectors that promote energy efficiency, resource regeneration, and ecological restoration. Every action taken within the economy is assessed for its potential to create continuity—whether by expanding renewable resources, protecting biodiversity, or enhancing the quality of life for all beings. By prioritizing life continuity, the system ensures that human progress aligns with the planet's natural rhythms, nurturing a world where economic growth supports—not undermines—the ability of future generations to thrive.

The Logic of Self-Regulation

To maintain coherence, this system operates on self-regulating principles. By establishing clear boundaries on value, the economy creates a finite dimension within which all activity is balanced and proportional. The burn-generate mechanism becomes crucial here, serving as an automatic check against excess or imbalance. When resources are consumed for economic growth, they are measured against the system's regenerative capacity, ensuring that no action creates a deficit that cannot be naturally restored.

This self-regulation not only prevents the destructive cycles of inflation and scarcity that characterize traditional economic systems but also fosters collective accountability. Every action, from production to consumption, is measured against its contribution to the whole, creating a sense of shared responsibility that drives individuals, businesses, and nations to think beyond short-term gains.

Conclusion: A New Paradigm of Economic Logic

The logic behind this system is simple yet transformative: value lies in continuity, creation, and coexistence. By aligning economic incentives with the natural processes of regeneration, this model envisions a future where humanity no longer drains its world to create progress. Instead, progress is defined by humanity's capacity to nurture, protect, and expand the resources that sustain life. In this vision, growth is not a race to consume but a cycle of creating conditions that support enduring prosperity for all.

The logic of this system is revolutionary, yet it taps into something innately human—a recognition that prosperity, at its core, is not about accumulation but about the continuity of life. By fostering a model that respects this truth, we can redefine what it means to thrive, not just today but for generations to come.

A COMPOSITE VALUE METRIC SYSTEM: A HOLISTIC APPROACH TO CURRENCY VALUATION

The Medium Value Currency (MVC) system introduces a revolutionary approach to valuing currency by tying it to a comprehensive composite value metric system. Unlike traditional currency systems that rely heavily on factors like supply and demand or speculative market forces, the MVC system is based on a Medium Value Index (MVI), which evaluates a country's overall performance across several critical dimensions. These include innovation, economic activity, human development, ecological impact, social stability, as well as the population-to-growth ratio, circulating supply to MVI value ratio, supply and demand, reserves, and natural supplies.

This composite system offers a holistic measure of a country's value, encouraging nations to prioritize sustainable development, better governance, and human capital investment. Each metric plays a unique role in shaping a country's exchange rate relative to the MVC, ultimately driving growth and value creation in a way that reflects the true underpinnings of a nation's economy and societal well-being.

1. Innovation

Innovation is one of the central pillars of the MVI. It measures a country's ability to create and adopt new technologies, foster research and development, and support entrepreneurship and creative industries. Innovation drives economic growth, enhances productivity, and leads to the development of new industries that can significantly increase a nation's global economic standing.

- **Impact on Currency Value:** Countries that excel in innovation typically enjoy stronger exchange rates within the MVC system. By producing cutting-edge technologies, fostering startups, and investing in research, these nations contribute to global progress and increase their economic value.
- **Incentive for Development:** The MVC system encourages countries to invest in research and development, education, and technological infrastructure. The more a nation supports innovation, the higher its MVI score, enabling it to gain better access to resources and improve its currency strength.

2. Economic Activity

Economic activity encompasses a country's gross domestic product (GDP), industrial output, trade volumes, and overall market dynamism. While this metric is often the foundation of traditional currency valuation, in the MVC system, it is only one of several key factors. This broad metric assesses how productive a country is across various sectors, from manufacturing and agriculture to services and technology.

- **Impact on Currency Value:** Strong economic activity ensures a nation's economic stability, contributing to a favorable exchange rate against the MVC. Nations with robust trade balances, high productivity, and diversified economies score higher on the MVI, making their currencies more competitive in the global marketplace.
- **Incentive for Development:** The system encourages countries to develop diversified economies, invest in industrial capacity, and improve trade relations. By promoting economic dynamism and reducing reliance on a single sector, nations can achieve higher MVI scores, further boosting their global currency position.

3. Human Development

Human development is a key metric that reflects a country's investment in its people. It includes factors like education, healthcare, life expectancy, literacy rates, and overall quality of life. Human development focuses on creating an environment where individuals can realize their full potential, contributing to the workforce and the economy.

- **Impact on Currency Value:** Countries that invest in education, healthcare, and social welfare improve their MVI score. Strong human capital leads to higher productivity and innovation, which in turn raises a nation's global economic standing and strengthens its currency.
- **Incentive for Development:** The MVC system encourages nations to prioritize human development by making it a significant factor in currency valuation. Countries with higher levels of education, healthier populations, and greater social mobility are rewarded with stronger currencies, pushing governments to implement policies that foster long-term human capital growth.

4. Ecological Impact

Ecological impact measures a country's environmental sustainability and resource management practices. This includes carbon emissions, renewable energy adoption, pollution control, and the preservation of natural resources. With growing global concern over climate change and environmental degradation, this metric encourages countries to adopt sustainable practices that protect the planet for future generations.

- **Impact on Currency Value:** Nations that prioritize environmental sustainability and reduce their ecological footprint score higher in the MVI, directly influencing their currency's value. The system incentivizes countries to engage in green initiatives, such as reducing emissions, adopting renewable energy sources, and protecting biodiversity, by rewarding them with stronger exchange rates.

- **Incentive for Development:** The MVC system encourages sustainable growth by linking a country's environmental responsibility to its economic value. Countries that implement policies to combat climate change, reduce waste, and conserve natural resources gain a competitive advantage in the global currency system.

5. Social Stability

Social stability encompasses a country's internal peace, governance quality, rule of law, and the strength of its civil institutions. Countries with strong governance, low crime rates, effective legal systems, and high levels of civic participation score well in this area. Social stability is crucial for maintaining investor confidence and ensuring long-term economic growth.

- **Impact on Currency Value:** Countries that are politically stable, have low levels of corruption, and strong legal frameworks see their MVI scores improve, leading to stronger currency valuations. Stability is essential for economic activity and investment, and nations that maintain peace and order are more attractive in the global economy.
- **Incentive for Development:** By rewarding social stability, the MVC system encourages governments to invest in political transparency, reduce corruption, and

promote civil rights. A stable and just society fosters economic growth, innovation, and long-term prosperity, contributing to a higher MVI score and better currency performance.

6. Population-to-Growth Ratio

The population-to-growth ratio is a critical factor that reflects the balance between a country's population growth and its ability to support that population through economic expansion and resource management. Rapid population growth without corresponding economic development can strain resources, whereas stable growth that matches economic capacity leads to sustainable development.

- **Impact on Currency Value:** Countries with a well-managed population-to-growth ratio, where population growth is supported by economic activity, infrastructure, and social services, see higher MVI scores. This balance ensures that economic development keeps pace with population needs, which helps maintain currency stability.
- **Incentive for Development:** The system encourages nations to focus on sustainable population growth by investing in family planning, education, and healthcare while ensuring that economic growth supports the increasing population. Countries that manage this ratio well gain currency strength, while those that fail to keep economic development in line with population growth risk lower MVI scores.

7. Circulating Supply to MVI Ratio

The circulating supply to MVI ratio ensures that a country's currency supply is proportional to its real economic value. This metric balances a country's money supply with its performance on the MVI, preventing inflation and ensuring that currency issuance aligns with actual economic growth and stability.

- **Impact on Currency Value:** Countries that maintain a balanced circulating supply in proportion to their MVI score will see stable currency valuations. This balance prevents overprinting of money, which can lead to inflation, and ensures that the currency's value is tied to real-world economic contributions.
- **Incentive for Development:** The MVC system forces governments to carefully manage currency issuance by linking it directly to the MVI. Nations that overprint money relative to their MVI performance will see excess currency burned to restore balance, encouraging responsible fiscal management and sustainable economic practices.

8. Supply and Demand

Supply and demand remains a fundamental economic principle within the MVC system, though it is now framed in the broader context of the MVI. This metric evaluates how a country's goods, services, and currency are demanded globally and how well the country can supply them. It reflects a nation's trade balance, resource availability, and market competitiveness.

- **Impact on Currency Value:** Strong global demand for a country's goods and services, combined with efficient supply chains, positively influences the MVI score, improving the country's currency valuation. Conversely, imbalances in supply and demand can weaken the currency and lower the nation's global standing.
- **Incentive for Development:** The system incentivizes countries to improve their trade practices, streamline production, and enhance market competitiveness. Countries that balance their supply and demand efficiently are rewarded with stronger currencies in the global exchange.

9. Reserves

Reserves refer to the financial and resource reserves a country holds, including foreign exchange reserves, gold, and other assets. A strong reserve position reflects economic resilience and the ability to manage economic downturns and external shocks.

- **Impact on Currency Value:** Countries with significant reserves score higher on the MVI, as reserves offer security and stability in times of economic uncertainty. A nation's reserve position directly influences its ability to manage currency value and maintain investor confidence.
- **Incentive for Development:** The MVC system encourages countries to build and maintain strong reserves, ensuring they have the necessary financial

backing to support their currency and economic infrastructure during periods of volatility. This leads to greater long-term stability and stronger currency performance.

10. Natural Supplies

Natural supplies encompass a nation's access to and sustainable management of its natural resources, including energy reserves, water, minerals, and arable land. In the MVC system, this metric recognizes the importance of ecological wealth and responsible resource utilization as a foundation for long-term economic and environmental stability.

- **Impact on Currency Value:** Nations with abundant and sustainably managed natural supplies secure a stable foundation for economic resilience and ecological balance. Their ability to responsibly harness and preserve resources boosts their MVI score, contributing to a stronger and more competitive currency position in the global marketplace.
- **Incentive for Sustainability:** The MVC system encourages nations to adopt sustainable resource management practices, invest in renewable energy, and protect critical ecosystems. By promoting resource conservation and reducing dependency on non-renewable supplies, countries can achieve higher MVI scores, securing long-term economic and environmental benefits.

This approach ties currency valuation to a nation's commitment to safeguarding its natural supplies, aligning economic growth with ecological responsibility.

Conclusion: A Holistic Approach to Currency Valuation

By integrating these ten key metrics into the Medium Value Index (MVI), the MVC system offers a truly holistic measure of a country's economic value, moving beyond the narrow focus of traditional currency systems. Countries are incentivized to improve across these multiple dimensions—whether in innovation, human development, or ecological sustainability—leading to better governance, sustainable growth, and a more equitable global economy. The MVC not only redefines how we understand currency but also reshapes the way nations approach growth and value creation in the 21st century.

THE MEDIUM VALUE CURRENCY (MVC) AS A GLOBAL STANDARD

In the contemporary global economy, the U.S. dollar serves as the primary world reserve currency, facilitating international trade and financial transactions. However, this reliance on a single national currency introduces risks and imbalances, as it ties global stability to the economic performance of one country. The Medium Value Currency (MVC) offers a solution to this issue by establishing a new global standard, where currency value is based on a comprehensive Medium Value Index (MVI) rather than the strength of any one nation's economy.

Unlike the U.S. dollar, which is directly linked to the performance of the U.S. economy, the MVC is backed by the combined global value, as measured by the MVI. This index evaluates countries on a broad range of metrics—including innovation, human development, ecological impact, social stability, GDP, and economic activity—to determine their relative currency value. By linking currencies to the MVI, the MVC system creates a more stable and equitable global exchange platform, where every country's currency reflects its real contributions to the world economy.

Exchange Rates Based on MVI Performance

In the MVC system, national currencies are exchanged based on their relative value to the Medium Value Index (MVI). The exchange rate of a country's currency against the MVC is determined by the country's performance on the composite index, which reflects its overall standing across key dimensions of innovation, sustainability, human development, and more.

- **Performance-Based Valuation:** A country's MVI score directly influences its exchange rate against the MVC. Countries that excel in metrics like technological advancement, social stability, and environmental sustainability will have stronger exchange rates, making their national currencies more valuable in the global marketplace.
- **Encouraging Improvement:** This system incentivizes countries to improve their performance across all MVI metrics to enhance their exchange rate and strengthen their economic position. As countries invest in sustainable growth, governance, and social

development, they are rewarded with higher MVI scores and more favorable exchange rates.

Facilitating Smooth International Trade with MVC

The Medium Value Exchange (MVE) plays a pivotal role in ensuring smooth international trade and financial transactions. Under the MVC system, countries and businesses would exchange their national currencies for MVC in a manner similar to how they currently use the U.S. dollar or Euro. However, because the MVC is backed by global value, it offers a more resilient and neutral medium of exchange for cross-border transactions.

- **Cross-Border Transactions:** The MVE facilitates the seamless exchange of currencies for the MVC, ensuring stability and reducing the risks associated with currency volatility. This creates a more predictable environment for international trade, as businesses can transact in a currency that reflects the collective global economy, rather than being tied to the performance of any one country.
- **Currency Stability:** By exchanging national currencies for MVC, countries can reduce exposure to the fluctuations of traditional reserve currencies like the U.S. dollar, which can be subject to domestic economic instability. The MVC provides a more stable and reliable option for international transactions.

Generating and Burning Currency: Regulating National Supply

A key innovation in the MVC system is the use of burn/generate mechanisms to regulate the supply of national currencies in accordance with each country's performance on the MVI. These mechanisms ensure that the national currency supply remains in balance with economic conditions and global value contributions, preventing inflation or deflation while promoting stability.

Generating National Currency

When a country exchanges MVC back into its national currency, the generate mechanism allows for the creation of new currency units, but only if the equivalent amount of MVC is available. This ensures that the generation of new currency is backed by real value stored in the MVC.

- **Value-Linked Currency Creation:** The generation process ensures that any new currency created is tied directly to the MVI value of the country. This prevents governments from printing money arbitrarily and promotes responsible fiscal management. Currency creation is only permitted when a country's MVI score justifies the expansion of its money supply, preventing runaway inflation and maintaining the currency's value.
- **Supporting Growth:** The generate mechanism also supports economic expansion. As a country's economy grows and its MVI score improves, the system can generate additional currency units in line with that growth, ensuring that the money supply remains

proportional to the country's economic and social value.

Burning National Currency

Conversely, when a national currency is exchanged back into MVC, the burn mechanism removes an equivalent amount of national currency from circulation.

- **Economic Balance:** The system's burn mechanism ensures that the money supply is always aligned with the MVI, keeping the currency's value stable and reducing the risk of economic imbalances.

Incentivizing Global Investment and Cooperation

The burn/generate mechanisms in the MVC system also create opportunities for currency investment based on predicted MVI development. Countries that demonstrate potential for improvement—whether through innovation, human development, or ecological practices—become attractive targets for investment, as their MVI scores are likely to rise, strengthening their currency and economy.

- **Encouraging Investments in Developing** Economies: More advanced economies are incentivized to invest in developing nations to help them improve their MVI scores. By investing in infrastructure, education, and technology, stronger nations can support sustainable growth in developing countries. As these countries' MVI scores rise, both parties benefit from stronger currency values and more balanced global economic growth.

- **Fostering International Cooperation:** The MVC system encourages international cooperation by aligning the interests of more developed nations with those of developing countries. Investing in a country's MVI improvement not only strengthens the global economy but also contributes to global stability, sustainability, and social progress.

Regulatory Mechanisms and Inflation/Deflation Control

The burn/generate mechanisms also serve as critical tools in regulating inflationary and deflationary pressures within a country's economy. By ensuring that the national currency supply is always in balance with MVI performance, the system maintains economic stability.

- **Inflationary Regulation:** When excess national currency is burned, inflation is brought under control, as the supply of money is reduced to match the country's actual economic output. This prevents governments from inflating their economies through overprinting of currency and ensures that the value of money remains stable.
- **Deflationary Control:** Conversely, the generate mechanism allows for controlled currency creation when economic growth justifies it, preventing deflation and ensuring that the money supply expands in proportion to the country's economic contributions.

Conclusion: A Sustainable Global Currency for the Future

The Medium Value Currency (MVC) system represents a transformative shift in how global economies interact, exchange value, and regulate their currency supplies. By linking currency creation to MVI performance, the MVC system promotes sustainability, innovation, and responsible governance, while providing a stable global medium for cross-border trade.

The burn/generate mechanisms embedded in the MVE ensure that national currency supplies remain balanced, preventing inflation and deflation, while creating opportunities for global investment and economic cooperation. In this way, the MVC not only provides a more equitable and resilient alternative to traditional reserve currencies but also fosters a future where economic value is truly reflective of a nation's contributions to the world.

THE MVC BORROWING MECHANISM

The Medium Value Currency (MVC) system introduces a transformative global borrowing mechanism that combines stability, fairness, and sustainability. Unlike traditional financial systems, which fluctuate interest rates based on risk or geopolitical factors, the MVC system maintains a fixed interest rate for all borrowers, ensuring equal access to financial resources. Interest payments not only sustain the Medium Value Index Authority (MVIA) but also prevent arbitrary currency creation, making the MVC a value-backed currency. Additionally, the system incorporates a generate/burn mechanism, enabling nations to borrow without system inflation. This chapter delves into how borrowing works within the MVC system, the functionality of loans, and how excess interest payments contribute to global support projects and an emergency global fund, supporting both long-term stability and global welfare.

Fixed Interest and Value-Backed Currency

At the heart of the MVC borrowing mechanism is the principle of equal access to capital through a fixed interest rate applied to all borrowers, regardless of their MVI score. Whether a country excels in global performance metrics or is in the early stages of improvement, the borrowing cost remains the same. This guarantees financial predictability and removes biases often present in traditional lending systems.

What sets the MVC apart is that interest payments are used to sustain the system itself. Instead of creating new currency arbitrarily, the MVC is supported by the interest generated through borrowing. This ensures that every unit of MVC in circulation is backed by real economic activity, preventing inflationary pressures. The MVC system also introduces future loans, allowing countries to borrow based on expected improvements in their MVI scores. This proactive borrowing approach helps nations fund projects that will elevate their performance and achieve long-term growth.

Borrowing Limits Tied to Performance (MVI)

While the interest rate is uniform, the borrowing capacity within the MVC system is determined by a country's MVI score, which reflects its performance in areas such as economic growth, sustainability, and social stability. Higher-performing countries enjoy greater borrowing limits, giving them more financial resources to invest in their development.

High MVI Score: Countries with strong MVI scores can borrow larger amounts relative to their GDP, which they can invest in large-scale projects such as infrastructure, technology, and social programs.

Lower MVI Score: Nations with lower MVI scores are still able to borrow, but with stricter limits to prevent over-leveraging and ensure responsible use of resources.

Interest Payments Sustaining the MVC System

A core feature of the MVC system is that interest payments from loans provide the primary funding for the MVIA, replacing the need for arbitrary currency creation. This ensures that the MVC remains a value-backed currency, underpinned by real economic activity and repayment of loans. Every unit of MVC is directly tied to a productive loan cycle, further stabilizing the currency's value.

Beyond simply funding the MVIA, excess interest payments are used to contribute to global support projects and the emergency global fund. This dual allocation ensures that the MVC system not only sustains itself but also actively participates in global development and crisis management:

Global Support Projects: A portion of excess interest funds is allocated to global initiatives such as sustainable energy, global healthcare improvements, and poverty reduction projects. By doing so, the MVC system contributes to the collective progress of the global community.

Emergency Global Fund: Excess interest also funds a global emergency reserve that can be rapidly deployed to address urgent situations such as natural disasters, pandemics, or humanitarian crises. This makes the MVC system not just a financial tool but a force for global resilience and security.

The Generate Mechanism

The generate mechanism within the MVC system is a critical innovation that regulates the supply of national currencies in relation to MVC borrowing. When a country borrows MVC or exchanges MVC for its national currency, the corresponding amount of national currency is generated, ensuring that liquidity is available for development projects. When loans are repaid, the generate mechanism works in reverse, as the national currency is burned, ensuring that excess liquidity does not destabilize the economy.

The generate mechanism also plays a vital role in the loan process. Upon repayment, the initial loan amount is burned to prevent inflationary effects, while the interest remains, supporting global projects and ensuring the system's sustainability. This balance between currency generation and destruction ensures that economic stability is maintained at all times.

Performance-Driven Borrowing Conditions

Although the interest rate is fixed, borrowing within the MVC system is still guided by performance-driven conditions based on a country's MVI score. This score determines both the amount a country can borrow and the flexibility of repayment terms.

High-Performing Countries: Nations with higher MVI scores can borrow larger sums and benefit from flexible repayment terms, such as extended grace periods or longer loan durations. This encourages nations to continually improve their MVI scores to gain better borrowing conditions.

Lower-Performing Countries: While still able to borrow, countries with lower MVI scores face tighter borrowing conditions and shorter repayment schedules to ensure that funds are used effectively to improve their metrics.

Borrowing in MVC Units

One of the unique features of the MVC system is that borrowing takes place in MVC units, aligning global financial transactions with a universal currency standard. By borrowing in MVC units, countries gain access to a global currency that is directly tied to their performance through the MVI system.

This borrowing structure ensures that the value of the MVC remains tied to real-world productivity, economic health, and social progress. As countries repay their loans in MVC or equivalent national currency, the system reinforces the integrity and value of the currency on a global scale.

Development-Oriented Loans for Lower MVI Scores

The MVC system ensures that even countries with lower MVI scores are not left behind. Development-oriented loans are available to help these nations invest in projects that will directly improve their performance in areas such as education, healthcare, infrastructure, and sustainability. These loans are subject to the same interest rate as all other loans but come with conditions that ensure the funds are used to create long-term value.

By facilitating access to capital for countries that need it most, the MVC system supports a more equitable global financial landscape, where all nations have the opportunity to improve their standing and contribute to global growth.

Global Support Projects and Emergency Funds

In addition to sustaining the MVIA, excess interest payments are used for global support projects and an emergency global fund. These funds ensure that the MVC system plays a crucial role in global development and crisis management.

Global Support Projects: Excess interest is invested in initiatives that provide global benefits, such as clean energy infrastructure, international education programs, and healthcare advancements. These projects not only improve the global economy but also enhance the well-being of societies worldwide.

Emergency Global Fund: A portion of excess interest is reserved for emergencies, providing rapid financial assistance during natural disasters, pandemics, or geopolitical crises. This ensures that the MVC system remains a force for good in times of global need, promoting resilience and recovery.

The MVC borrowing mechanism presents a groundbreaking system that ensures fairness, stability, and global responsibility. By applying a fixed interest rate, the MVC offers equal access to borrowing, while future loans allow countries to borrow against anticipated improvements in their MVI scores. The generate mechanism carefully regulates currency supply by burning the initial loan amount upon repayment, ensuring that liquidity remains balanced and inflation is controlled.

Interest payments not only sustain the MVC system but also contribute to global support projects and an emergency global fund, ensuring that the system benefits both borrowers and the global community. By combining performance-driven borrowing limits with development-oriented loans, the MVC system encourages sustainable growth and responsible financial management on a global scale. Ultimately, the MVC system offers a blueprint for a value-backed, equitable, and resilient financial system that promotes global well-being.

Implementing the MVIA: A Comprehensive Global Regulatory Framework

The introduction of the Medium Value Currency (MVC) as a global exchange unit and reserve currency requires more than just a revolutionary concept. To ensure the success of this system, a comprehensive international regulatory framework must be established. This framework will ensure that the system operates with fairness, transparency, and stability, promoting trust among nations and ensuring that currency valuation accurately reflects the real contributions of each country to the global economy.

At the center of this regulatory framework is the Medium Value Index Authority (MVIA), an international governance body responsible for overseeing the integrity of the MVC system. The MVIA will play a critical role in regulating the system, collecting and verifying data, ensuring compliance, and maintaining global transparency. Its operations will set the foundation for a stable and equitable global currency system that fosters sustainable growth and international cooperation.

MVIA: The Pillar of Global Regulation

The Medium Value Index Authority (MVIA) will function as the regulatory backbone of the MVC system, ensuring that all participating countries adhere to the principles and standards of the Medium Value Index (MVI). The MVIA will oversee the accurate measurement and implementation of MVI metrics across nations, ensuring that the composite index is applied fairly and consistently.

- **Global Governance:** The MVIA will act as an impartial global governance body, free from the influence of individual nations. Its role is to maintain the objectivity and integrity of the MVI, ensuring that all data collected from participating countries is standardized and reflects true economic and social value.
- **Regulation of Exchange Dynamics:** The MVIA will be responsible for managing the Medium Value Exchange (MVE), overseeing the burn/generate mechanisms and ensuring that national currencies are exchanged for MVC in line with MVI performance. By regulating currency flows, the MVIA ensures that the money supply remains balanced, preventing inflation and deflation and promoting global stability.

Ensuring Fairness, Transparency, and Stability

To build trust in the MVC system and encourage global adoption, the MVIA will establish rigorous standards to ensure fairness, transparency, and stability. These standards will guide the operation of the MVC system and prevent any form of manipulation or misrepresentation.

1. Standardized Data Collection and Reporting

One of the core responsibilities of the MVIA will be to establish standardized methods for data collection and reporting across all participating countries. This will ensure that each country's MVI score is calculated based on accurate and consistent information, preventing any discrepancies in how metrics are measured or reported.

- **Comparability Across Nations:** By using standardized data collection processes, the MVIA ensures that the performance metrics of one country can be directly compared with another's. This creates a level playing field, where all nations are judged by the same criteria and manipulation is avoided.
- **Transparent Reporting:** The MVIA will require countries to make data available to the public through regular reporting channels. This transparency builds trust in the system and allows independent verification of MVI scores, ensuring that all currency exchanges and valuations are based on reliable data.

2. Regular Audits and Public Data Access

To maintain the integrity of the MVC system, the MVIA will conduct regular audits of the data submitted by participating countries. These audits will ensure that countries are complying with the system's guidelines and that their MVI scores are an accurate reflection of their real economic and social performance.

- **Preventing Manipulation:** Regular audits will prevent countries from artificially inflating their MVI scores by manipulating data or misreporting performance metrics. The audit process will be transparent and impartial, protecting the credibility of the MVC system.
- **Public Accountability:** The MVIA will provide public access to audit results and MVI data. This public access ensures that the global community can hold governments accountable, further enhancing the system's transparency and trustworthiness.

3. Incentives for Compliance and Sanctions for Non-Compliance

To encourage full participation in the MVC system and ensure compliance with the rules, the MVIA will implement a system of rewards and penalties. Compliance will be incentivized through benefits such as favorable exchange rates, while non-compliance will be penalized through sanctions or other restrictions.

- **Rewards for High Performance:** Countries that comply with the MVI framework and demonstrate consistent improvement in their MVI scores will be rewarded with stronger exchange rates and increased global standing. These incentives will encourage nations to invest in sustainable practices, human development, and innovation.

- **Penalties for Non-Compliance:** Countries that fail to adhere to the system's guidelines or that misreport data will face sanctions, which could include reduced access to the MVC system, weaker exchange rates, or exclusion from certain global financial agreements. These penalties will ensure that all participants follow the rules and contribute to the system's success.

Adaptation to Evolving Global Needs

The MVIA will be designed to adapt to the changing needs of the global economy. As the world evolves, new challenges and opportunities will emerge, requiring the MVC system to remain flexible and responsive. To ensure this adaptability, the MVIA will conduct regular reviews of the MVI framework and make adjustments as needed to reflect new global realities.

- **Evolving Metrics:** As global priorities shift—such as increasing focus on climate change, technological advancement, or population growth—the MVIA will update the MVI metrics to ensure that the currency system continues to reflect the most important indicators of national and global health.
- **Continuous Improvement:** The MVIA will remain engaged with international organizations, academic institutions, and other stakeholders to continuously refine the MVI model. This will allow the system to stay at the forefront of global economic regulation and remain relevant in a rapidly changing world.

Digital Platform for MVI Management

Given the complexity of managing a global currency system, the MVIA will maintain a secure digital platform to facilitate MVI activities. This platform will serve as the central hub for managing data submissions, conducting MVI calculations, and facilitating the burn/generate mechanisms.

- **Secure and Efficient Operations:** The platform will be equipped with state-of-the-art security to protect sensitive data and ensure the integrity of all financial transactions. This digital infrastructure will streamline currency exchanges and ensure that the MVI system operates smoothly and efficiently on a global scale.
- **Accessible Data and Reporting:** The platform will provide real-time data access to participating nations and the global public, offering insights into MVI scores, currency valuations, and the overall health of the MVC system. This accessibility enhances transparency and trust in the system.

Collaboration with International Organizations

The MVIA will collaborate closely with existing international organizations such as the International Monetary Fund (IMF), World Bank, and United Nations, among others. These partnerships will help align the MVC system with global standards and ensure that it complements other international financial frameworks.

- **Harmonizing Global Standards:** By working with established international organizations, the MVIA will ensure that the MVC system aligns with existing financial and economic regulations. This collaboration will also promote global cooperation and make the transition to the MVC smoother for participating nations.

Educational Support and Capacity Building

To ensure that all countries, particularly developing nations, can effectively participate in the MVI system, the MVIA will offer educational programs and capacity-building support. This will help nations strengthen their ability to collect accurate data, manage their currency exchanges, and improve their MVI scores.

- **Educational Initiatives:** The MVIA will offer training programs for government officials, economists, and data specialists to help them understand and implement the MVI system. This will ensure that all participating countries have the knowledge and resources needed to fully engage with the system.
- **Capacity Building:** Developing nations will receive additional support to help them build the infrastructure necessary for collecting accurate data, managing their economy, and improving their MVI performance. This support will help these countries achieve higher MVI scores and benefit more fully from the MVC system.

Conclusion: A Stable, Transparent, and Fair Global Currency System

The implementation of the Medium Value Currency (MVC) requires the creation of a robust international regulatory framework overseen by the Medium Value Index Authority (MVIA). Through its responsibilities for data collection, auditing, and enforcement, the MVIA will ensure the fairness, transparency, and stability of the MVC system. With standardized reporting methods, regular audits, and public access to data, the system will operate with integrity, fostering trust among nations.

The MVIA will also adapt to evolving global needs, ensuring the MVC system remains relevant and responsive to future challenges. By providing educational support and collaborating with international organizations, the MVIA will help nations fully participate in the system, promoting global economic stability and cooperation. Through these efforts, the MVC system will lay the foundation for a more equitable, transparent, and sustainable global economy.

TRANSITION TO MVC: A STRATEGIC TWO-PHASE PATHWAY TO GLOBAL ECONOMIC STABILITY

The Medium Value Currency (MVC) system represents a revolutionary shift from a dollar-centric global economy to a sustainable, balanced framework where value is measured by collective productivity, sustainability, and real economic health. To facilitate this transition while leveraging the U.S.'s strong position within the existing system, a two-phase approach provides a structured pathway that allows the U.S. to manage its international debt obligations effectively while gradually shifting global economic reliance toward MVC.

This comprehensive plan combines both strategic and operational elements to ensure that the transition happens smoothly and equitably, addressing the interests of the U.S. while establishing a globally representative standard of value.

Phase 1: Gradual Integration with U.S. Exceptions

The Medium Value Currency (MVC) system offers a transformative shift from a dollar-centric global economy to a more sustainable, balanced framework where value is determined by collective productivity, sustainability, and true economic health. This transition relies on a two-phase approach that leverages the U.S.'s unique position within the current system, allowing it to manage international debt obligations effectively while guiding global reliance towards the MVC framework.

This comprehensive approach combines both strategic and operational elements to ensure a smooth and equitable transition that considers U.S. interests while establishing a new, globally representative standard of value.

Phase 1: Gradual Integration and Conditional Conversion

In the first phase, the U.S. retains some flexibility in managing debt, allowing it to make payments in dollars but with a significant shift—any dollar-based debt payments are contingent upon the receiving country's willingness to convert these payments into MVC. This structure mitigates sudden disruptions while providing the time needed for global markets to adapt to the MVC network.

1. **Conditional Debt Payments with MVC Conversion Requirement:** In this phase, the U.S. continues making debt payments in dollars. However, any country choosing to receive these payments must convert the dollar holdings into MVC. The conversion process relies on the U.S.'s Medium Value Index (MVI) score, reflecting productivity, sustainability, and economic health, ensuring a fair value exchange as dollar reserves shift toward MVC.

2. **Controlled Conversion and Burning Mechanism:** As countries convert dollar reserves into MVC under the contingency model, the conversion rate aligns with the U.S.'s MVI score, linking debt repayment to sustainable economic metrics. Converted dollars are then "burned" to reduce dollar liquidity in global markets, preventing inflationary pressures and maintaining stability while the U.S. manages debt.

3. **Dual-Network Flexibility for Trade and Transactions:** A dual-network structure enables countries to conduct trade within either MVC or dollar systems. This option allows for gradual migration of liquidity toward MVC, building trust and fostering a smooth transition as global entities become familiar with MVC-based transactions, gradually reducing dependency on the dollar.

Phase 2: Locking Value and Finalizing the Transition to MVC

In the second phase, all participating countries, including the U.S., fully integrate into the MVC framework, locking currency values within a fixed, MVI-driven system. This phase completes the transition, moving global reliance from the dollar to the MVC standard.

1. **Full MVI-Based Value Lock:** In Phase 2, all currencies are secured within the MVC framework. Each currency's value is strictly tied to MVI-based metrics, eliminating dollar-based debt issuance flexibility and requiring all participants to adhere to MVC standards. This value lock fosters a balanced global economy, preventing excessive currency creation.

2. **Complete Currency Conversion and Burning of Remaining Dollar Reserves:** With dollar-based debt payments phased out, any remaining dollar reserves are fully converted to MVC and burned. This eliminates the dollar's dominant role, securing MVC as the primary global reserve. The conversion and burning mechanism ensures inflation control, stabilizing liquidity across markets.

3. **Incentivizing Sustainable Global Cooperation:** By locking value within the MVI-based MVC system, countries have an intrinsic motivation to maintain high MVI scores to enhance their currency's worth. This promotes sustainable development and shifts economic focus toward shared global stability and resilience.

4. **A Balanced and Independent Global Economy:** With the dollar phased out as the default reserve, the MVC system achieves currency neutrality. Independence from any single nation's currency promotes stability and inclusivity, ensuring that economic power is equitably distributed. The MVC framework's reliance on MVI metrics ties value to real productivity and sustainability, reducing vulnerability to fluctuations in individual nations and fostering a balanced global economy.

The MVC system thus provides a structured, strategic pathway from a dollar-centered system to a sustainability-based, globally inclusive model. Through conditional debt conversion and gradual integration, this approach facilitates a smooth transition that reduces dependency on the dollar while establishing MVC as the foundation for a fair, resilient, and cooperative global economy.

Conclusion: MVC as the Foundation of a Sustainable Future

Through this comprehensive, two-phase approach, the MVC system offers a strategic pathway for the U.S. to alleviate its debt while transitioning the global economy to a stable, sustainable standard of value. The MVC network, grounded in MVI metrics, creates an inclusive economy where growth is aligned with the true needs of humanity and the environment, setting the stage for a prosperous, resilient future for all.

Through the initial phase, the system repurposes U.S. debt payments into a valuable asset within the MVC, counteracting inflation and grounding value in MVI-based metrics. The process not only limits inflationary pressures but also builds a foundation of trust in MVC, positioning it as a globally recognized standard for sustainable value. This phase transforms debt into a positive economic driver, ensuring that each dollar paid ultimately supports the world's economic stability and value growth through MVC.

The absorption of dollar value into MVC is the cornerstone of this system, creating a bridge from national currency to universal currency while retaining and redistributing real value. This method not only smooths the transition but also establishes MVC as a trusted, inflation-resistant global standard, backed by tangible economic contributions and ecological sustainability. The stored dollar value becomes the bedrock for a new era in global finance—one where value is as much about collective progress as it is about economic stability.

REDEFINING ECONOMIC VALUE: FROM PRODUCTION TO ACCESSIBLE GROWTH

For centuries, nations have measured economic success by the amount of output produced, focusing on metrics like Gross Domestic Product (GDP) to gauge growth. However, while economic output provides a snapshot of productivity, it fails to answer a critical question: Can people actually access the value created?

This chapter explores the distinction between increasing economic value produced and enhancing access to that value, emphasizing how access is essential for sustainable growth and inflation control. The Medium Value Currency (MVC) framework emerges as a transformative approach that redefines value through accessible growth, prioritizing quality of life and equitable prosperity. True value creation lies in economic access to growth and in fostering growth potential for all—not merely increasing output.

The Limits of Production-Focused Growth

Traditional economic models often equate progress with expanding GDP. When a nation's GDP rises, it is typically assumed that the economy is healthier and that individuals will benefit. However, this output-centric view overlooks a vital factor: without access to value, economic growth remains abstract and largely unattainable for many.

GDP and Value Produced: GDP per capita provides an average measure of economic output per person, suggesting that each citizen theoretically benefits from economic activity. However, GDP growth does not guarantee improved quality of life, especially if access to resources is limited. When GDP rises without an increase in individuals' ability to access goods and services, growth becomes uneven and ultimately unsustainable.

Disconnected from Real Impact: A focus on production can lead to growth that fails to reach the average person. Wealth concentration, rising living costs, and systemic inequality can prevent significant segments of the population from experiencing the benefits of growth. This disconnect becomes particularly problematic during inflationary periods, as higher production does not necessarily translate into more accessible value.

Access to Value as the Foundation of Sustainable Economic Health

An economy's true strength lies not just in what it produces but in how well people can access that production. Access to value is crucial for sustainable growth because it ensures that economic gains are distributed in ways that improve people's lives and stimulate economic participation.

Purchasing Power as Access: Purchasing power per capita is a critical metric for measuring real value, reflecting individuals' ability to buy goods and services while accounting for inflation and cost of living. Unlike GDP per capita, which measures output, purchasing power indicates the real impact of economic value, signaling whether incomes are increasing in ways that enhance quality of life.

Access-Driven Growth and Inflation Control: When individuals can effectively access value, they contribute to stable economic growth. Higher purchasing power leads to demand that aligns with production capacity, fostering a balanced economy where supply and demand are naturally matched. This balance limits inflation by ensuring that production is driven by genuine demand rather than speculative or artificially inflated growth.

MVC's Role: Enhancing Access to Create Sustainable Growth

The Medium Value Currency (MVC) framework recognizes that sustainable economic health depends on increasing access to value rather than simply focusing on output. By redefining the role of currency, MVC aims to create a system where value reflects real, accessible quality of life rather than being driven solely by market dynamics.

Currency as a Measure of Accessible Value: In the MVC system, currency value is intrinsically linked to sustainable productivity, collective prosperity, and life quality, emphasizing the enhancement of purchasing power. This ensures that currency remains stable and resilient, promoting growth by strengthening access to essential goods and services, which supports long-term economic stability.

Intrinsic Value Tied to Life Quality: Through the Medium Value Index (MVI), MVC incentivizes growth that directly enhances life quality. Countries with high MVI scores effectively improve access to value, indicating healthy economies where inflation is controlled by sustainable demand. By grounding currency in accessible productivity, MVC creates a system where growth is meaningful and resilient against inflationary pressures.

Access and Value Creation: A Partnership for Growth and Stability

When value creation is paired with enhanced access, economic growth becomes both sustainable and inflation-resistant. Accessible value is essential for building a resilient economy where individuals maintain consistent purchasing power and where demand naturally aligns with supply.

Building an Inclusive Economy: Access-driven value creation supports an economy that distributes benefits widely, reducing wealth concentration and ensuring that more people participate in growth. This inclusivity not only enhances quality of life but also strengthens the economy by fostering a stable consumer base that drives demand without generating inflationary pressure.

Access as an Inflation Control Mechanism: As more individuals access value, production aligns with actual demand, limiting the need for excessive monetary expansion. This balance helps prevent inflationary cycles and hyperinflation risks, often triggered by growth that is production-driven yet inaccessible. MVC's approach to currency supports this balance by ensuring that value is closely tied to accessible quality of life.

True Value Creation: Economic Access to Growth and Growth Potential

At its core, true value creation is about fostering economic access to growth and maximizing growth potential for all. This means not only increasing current purchasing power but also building an economic foundation that enables future generations to access resources, innovate, and contribute. When people have access to growth and the potential to expand it, economies become more resilient, equitable, and capable of sustained progress.

Creating Long-Term Growth Potential: By ensuring access to resources and opportunities, MVC encourages an environment where individuals and businesses can thrive, innovate, and grow. This focus on growth potential enables continuous economic renewal and stability, preparing the economy for future challenges.

Embedding Access into the Economic Fabric: With MVC, access to value is not an afterthought but a primary goal. By linking currency to sustainable, accessible value, MVC creates an economy where growth potential is distributed broadly, allowing more people to participate in and drive economic progress.

The Future of Economic Value: Redefining Growth by Access

MVC offers a new dimension of economic value, one where currency is a tool for enhancing access rather than merely facilitating transactions. In this system, economic growth is not measured solely by production but by how accessible and impactful that production is for the population.

Currency as a Reflection of Quality of Life: By redefining currency value through access, MVC aligns economic growth with human well-being. This reframing transforms currency from a speculative asset into a metric for life quality, ensuring that economic success is measured by real access and purchasing power.

A Stable Foundation for Global Prosperity: With access to value as its foundation, MVC builds an inclusive economic model where growth is distributed equitably. This approach supports inflation control, as currency stability derives from individuals' ability to afford what they need rather than from speculative or debt-driven expansion.

Conclusion: Access as the Cornerstone of Real Economic Value

The MVC approach moves beyond the limitations of production-focused growth to prioritize accessible value as the foundation of economic health. By pairing value creation with real access, MVC establishes a system where growth and stability go hand in hand. This shift from output to access is not merely an economic adjustment; it represents a redefinition of success, aligning economic priorities with human well-being.

In the MVC system, value is not just an abstract figure but something individuals can experience, afford, and use to improve their lives. By focusing on access, MVC ensures that currency reflects a resilient, inflation-resistant foundation for a prosperous, sustainable future. This approach builds a new economic dimension where currency is both a measure of life quality and a driver of collective prosperity—a system where growth is as accessible as it is real.

CONCLUSION

In this book, we have outlined a comprehensive vision for a new socio-economic system that integrates the social, governmental, and currency frameworks necessary to ensure a sustainable, equitable, and thriving global society. Each of these interconnected pillars contributes to a future where individual development, ethical governance, and global cooperation are prioritized.

Socioeconomic Framework

The proposed socioeconomic system emphasizes universal access to basic necessities such as healthcare, food security, and affordable housing. By ensuring these foundational needs are met, the system fosters individual growth and eliminates economic disparities that often hinder personal development. State custody of children and parental involvement reflect the commitment to nurturing future generations within a supportive framework, where parental training and family structures are aligned with societal goals.

This model not only seeks to improve individual lives but also aims to create a stable society where universal access to resources ensures that each citizen can contribute to and benefit from the broader social fabric.

Social Model

The social structure places human psychology and individual well-being at its core. By shifting the responsibility of child-rearing to the state, supported by comprehensive parental training, the system reduces stress and instability often associated with family dynamics, fostering an environment where children can thrive and individuals can fully engage with their own development.

This approach promotes mental health, reduces societal issues such as depression and isolation, and creates social cohesion. By offering an unconditional safety net with access to resources, the system encourages individuals to pursue personal fulfillment without the burden of survival pressures.

Governmental Model

At the heart of the governmental model is the Ethics Chamber, a body responsible for ensuring that all social, economic, and political decisions adhere to the highest standards of ethics and sustainability. This chamber oversees not only domestic policies but also international agreements, ensuring that decisions are aligned with long-term societal goals.

Currency and Economic Model

The introduction of the Medium Value Currency (MVC) system offers a revolutionary approach to global economic exchange. Unlike traditional currencies, the MVC is tied to the Medium Value Index (MVI), a composite measure that reflects a country's true value based on innovation, human development, ecological sustainability, and social stability.

The MVC serves as a global reserve currency, ensuring stability in international trade and incentivizing countries to improve their performance across multiple dimensions. The burn/generate mechanism regulates national currency supplies, maintaining economic balance by linking money creation to real-world contributions.

This model encourages nations to invest in sustainable practices and cooperate globally, fostering a future where economic value is more accurately represented and aligned with societal well-being.

A Vision for the Future

This integrated model of socioeconomic, social, governmental, and currency frameworks provides a blueprint for a more equitable, transparent, and sustainable society. By prioritizing individual development, ethical governance, and a currency system that reflects real value, this vision lays the foundation for a global society that thrives on cooperation, fairness, and progress.

The MVC system incentivizes nations to invest in their people and their planet, while the Ethics Chamber ensures that governance serves the collective good. Together, these systems work to eliminate disparities, promote human flourishing, and create a future where prosperity and fulfillment are achievable for all.

You Are the World

As we come to the end of this journey, there is one essential truth I want to leave you with: You are not just an extension of the world; you are the world. Each of us is not a passive participant in life, shaped solely by the forces around us. Rather, we are active contributors, and our thoughts, actions, and choices ripple out, influencing the entire fabric of reality.

You are a reflection of the world's complexity, diversity, and potential. Every decision you make, every path you choose, adds to the collective experience of humanity. By pursuing your autonomy, by seeking to understand your true self beyond the constraints of identity politics and societal labels, you are actively shaping the world around you.

Your journey toward self-realization is not just personal—it is deeply connected to the larger whole. The way you navigate your life, the way you express your unique identity, your values, and your aspirations—all of these shape not only your future but also the future of humanity.

Embracing this truth means recognizing that your quest for dignity and autonomy is not just about you; it's about the world we are all creating together. In every moment, with every choice, you have the power to uplift yourself and contribute to the greater good. You are part of something much larger than yourself, yet you are also a vital part of that whole.

So, as you move forward, remember: You are the world. You are the change. Your autonomy, your dignity, and your conscious participation in this life are what will shape the world to come. It is through you—through your choices, your actions, and your spirit—that the world evolves. You are not just in the world; you are the world, and the future is yours to shape.

COPING WITH LIFE – EMBRACING THE NOW

The essence of coping and healing lies in embracing the present moment. Life doesn't unfold in the past or the future—it happens *now*. By accepting this truth, we find liberation from the fears, regrets, and anxieties that bind us. To cope is to live fully, fearlessly, and authentically, acknowledging the impermanence of all things while finding peace in our fleeting existence. This chapter explores the key principles for coping with life and the transformative power of acceptance, fearlessness, and understanding.

1. You Only Live Now: Embracing the Present

The first step toward coping is recognizing that life only exists in the present. The past is a memory, the future an idea—neither can hold power over you unless you allow them to. By focusing on the present moment, you free yourself from the burdens of what has been and what might be.

In the present, you have the ability to choose how to live, how to respond, and how to experience the world. Each moment is an opportunity to shape your life according to your true desires, rather than being weighed down by past mistakes or future uncertainties. The more you stay connected to the present, the more fully you can experience life as it is happening, with all its beauty, pain, and potential.

2. Acceptance is Liberation

To truly cope with the challenges of life, you must embrace the power of *acceptance*. Acceptance is not resignation or passive submission; it is the active acknowledgment of what *is*. It means letting go of the need to control everything, to change the unchangeable, or to fight against reality.

When you accept life as it is—both the good and the bad—you find freedom. Acceptance allows you to release the suffering that comes from resisting reality. You understand that pain is part of life, but suffering is optional. By accepting your experiences, emotions, and circumstances, you open the door to healing and inner peace. In acceptance, you find liberation.

3. Fearlessness is Trust in Yourself and the Universe

Fearlessness does not mean the absence of fear—it means trusting in yourself and the universe even when fear arises. Fear is a natural response to the unknown, to change, and to the uncertainty of life. But fearlessness is the ability to move forward despite fear, to trust that you are capable of handling whatever life brings, and realizing nothing worse than death can happen to you.

Trusting in yourself means believing that you have the strength, resilience, and wisdom to cope with whatever challenges arise. Trusting in the universe means understanding that life is a constant flow, and while you cannot control everything, you can navigate life with grace and courage. Fearlessness is the quiet confidence that comes from knowing you are enough as you are, and that life is unfolding exactly as it should, even when it's hard to see.

4. Nothing Will Ever Last: Embracing Impermanence

One of the fundamental truths of life is that nothing lasts forever. Everything—people, emotions, experiences, circumstances—is in a constant state of change. To cope with life's inevitable ups and downs, you must embrace the impermanence of all things.

When you accept that nothing will ever last, you are freed from the fear of loss and the need for constant attachment. You learn to appreciate life's fleeting moments for what they are, rather than clinging to them out of fear. This understanding brings a sense of peace, as you realize that everything is temporary, and that's okay. In fact, it is this impermanence that makes life precious.

By embracing the transient nature of existence, you learn to live more fully in the present, appreciating each moment for what it is, knowing that it, too, will pass.

5. Enjoy and Become: Finding Joy in the Process

Life is not a destination—it is a journey of *becoming*. The more you focus on enjoying the process of living, the more meaningful and fulfilling your life becomes. To cope is to understand that joy is not found in the end result, but in the act of living itself.

Becoming is an ongoing process. Each day, each experience, each challenge shapes who you are and who you will become. The key is to find joy in the present moment, in the small things, and in the growth that comes from life's experiences. When you stop waiting for happiness to come in the future, and instead find it in the here and now, you unlock the true meaning of life.

6. Understanding is the First Step Toward Healing

Understanding is a powerful tool for healing and coping. When you seek to understand yourself—your emotions, your fears, your desires—you begin the journey toward self-compassion and healing. To understand is to illuminate the parts of yourself that may have been hidden or ignored, and it is through this illumination that healing begins.

Understanding also extends to the world around you. When you seek to understand others, you cultivate empathy and connection, which are essential for coping with life's challenges. By understanding that everyone is on their own journey of becoming, you let go of judgment and embrace acceptance—for yourself and for others.

Healing begins with understanding. It is the first step toward wholeness, allowing you to move forward with clarity, compassion, and self-awareness.

7. Self-Forgiveness and Impermanence:

Recognize that just as everything in life is impermanent, so too are your mistakes, regrets, and missteps. Holding onto guilt or shame only prolongs suffering. By understanding that nothing lasts forever—not even your past actions—you can release the need for self-punishment. Embrace the idea that you are constantly evolving, and that forgiveness is a natural part of that evolution. In the grand cycle of impermanence, each moment offers a fresh start, an opportunity to let go, learn, and move forward with compassion for yourself.

8. To Live, You Must Master the Art of Dying

The final truth of life is that to truly *live*, you must learn to embrace death. This doesn't mean fearing death, but understanding it as an inevitable part of life's cycle. The art of dying is not about physical death alone—it is about learning to let go of attachments, of identities, of the ego, and of the need for control.

In mastering the art of dying, you release the fear of the unknown and the need to cling to what is. You accept that life is a constant process of death and rebirth—of letting go and becoming anew. Each day, parts of your old self die, and new parts are born. This is the essence of growth.

To live fully is to understand that death is not an ending, but a transformation. It is a necessary part of life's journey, and by accepting it, you free yourself to live without fear. In mastering the art of dying, you master the art of living.

And Love...

Remember to Be You, You Only Live Now

In the journey of healing, integration, and self-discovery, the most important lesson is to *be you*. Embrace the complexities of your identity—the primal forces that drive your desires and instincts, as well as the refined constructs that shape your thoughts, values, and relationships. You are not defined by past traumas or rigid societal expectations; you are defined by the unique balance of these forces within yourself.

The present moment is where your true power lies. You only live *now*, and it is in this moment that you have the ability to reclaim your identity, rewrite your story, and live authentically. The past may have shaped you, but it does not have to confine you. The future is yet to be written, but it will be written by the choices you make today.

So, embrace who you are—raw, refined, complex, and evolving. Remember that life happens in the now, and it's in this present moment that you have the opportunity to live fully, express your true self, and find harmony between all the aspects of your identity. Be courageous, be authentic, and, above all, be you.

www.ingramcontent.com/pod-product-compliance
Lightning Source LLC
LaVergne TN
LVHW022310090825
818242LV00042B/1057